PARIS

THE ESSENTIAL CITY

PARIS
THE ESSENTIAL CITY

Godfrey Howard
Photographed by Françoise Legrand

David & Charles
Newton Abbot   London

Books by the same author:
Getting Through!
A Guide to the Loire Valley
Boatopia
A Guide to Good English in the 1980s

Howard, Godfrey
    Paris: the essential city/
    1. France. Paris. Visitors' guides
    I.   Title
    914.4'3604838

    ISBN 0-7153-9153-4

Typeset by ABM Typographics Limited Hull
and printed in Great Britain
by Butler & Tanner Limited, Frome, Somerset
for David & Charles Publishers plc
Brunel House   Newton Abbot   Devon

For Božidar and Grace,
and Sammy and Sonia,
and for Mary –
who all fell in love
in and with Paris

CONTENTS

ACKNOWLEDGEMENTS

I am grateful to the historians, curators, chefs and other busy people in Paris who took time off to give me help. Special thanks go to Pauline Hallam of the French Government Tourist Office, to Marc Jordan of *The Macmillan Dictionary of Art* for advice, to Lesley Howard for expert guidance over translations, to Tracey May at my publishers for so much consideration, and to Françoise Legrand for driving me round Paris with the dash and daring of a Parisian taxi-driver.

Acknowledgements are also made to the following for the use of short quotations from copyright material. As a courtesy, every effort was made to contact copyright holders and if there are any omissions or inaccuracies, please accept my apologies.

G.H.

John Calder (Publishers) Ltd., London and Grove Press Inc., New York: *Black Spring* by Henry Miller.

Jonathan Cape Ltd., London: *Enthusiasms* by Bernard Levin © 1983 (also Curtis Brown Ltd., London). *A Moveable Feast* by Ernest Hemingway (also Charles Scribner's Sons, New York and the Executors of the Ernest Hemingway Estate).

Harold P. Clunn, author of *The Face of Paris*.

Collins, London: *The French* by Theodore Zeldin.

Contrejour, Paris: *La Photographie Française* by Claude Nori.

André Deutsch, London: *Quartet* by Jean Rhys (also W. W. Norton, New York).

Éditions Bernard Grasset, Paris: *Pays Parisiens* by Daniel Halévy.

Expression: article by Frank Johnson.

Faber and Faber: *Cities* by Jan Morris; *Richard Rogers* by Brian Appleyard; *Shakespeare and Company* by Sylvia Beach.

Financial Times: articles by William Packer and Lucia van der Post.

The Guardian: articles by John Berger and Richard Gott.

The Independent: article by Elkan Allan and editorial.

London Evening Standard: articles by James Burstall, Jill Crawshaw and Fay Maschler.

Andy MacElhone: Harry's Bar 75th anniversary booklet.

Methuen and Co. Ltd.: *A Wanderer in Paris* by E. V. Lucas.

John Murray, London: *Civilisation* by Kenneth Clark (also BBC Publications and Harper and Row, New York).

The Observer: articles by William Feaver and Sam White.

The Spectator: article by Diana Mosley.

Thames and Hudson: *Paris* by John Russell; *France Observed* (Jean Cocteau and Lucien François).

Time Out: article by Kate Baillie.

THE ESSENTIAL CITY

Bozidar Kantuser is a Yugoslav composer who has lived and worked in Paris for more than half his life. When he arrived he knew little French and had even less money. He is now director of the International Library of Contemporary Music, which he founded in Paris, where he also met, and subsequently married, a New York painter, Grace Renzi, then a young hopeful 'American in Paris'. They live in a second-floor apartment in the heart of the city, overlooking the Pont Louis-Philippe and the Ile St-Louis. It is a small, rather cramped apartment, but to have breakfast every morning looking out over the Seine makes up for that.

One day I asked Bozidar when he first came to Paris.

'24 September 1950.' he answered.

'How is it you remember the exact day?'

'Because that's when it seemed life really began. And nobody forgets their birthday, do they? When you come to Paris, you never go back. You never look back.'

I turned to Grace, Bozidar's wife.

What about you Grace, when did *you* first come here?'

'Three years after Bozidar.'

'But why did you wait so long?'

'I didn't know that Paris and Bozidar were waiting for me.'

Paris has for so long been like a powerful magnet drawing to it artists, composers, writers, intellectuals and savants of all kinds. From all over the western world they have come to Paris the way Mohammedans go to Mecca, as if to a shrine, to a fount of inspiration where ideas and the expression of creative talent can flower and flourish as nowhere else. Napoleon believed that Paris was the one city in the world where you could stretch your abilities to the limits.

That is what Paris has become for so many people, the great formative influence in their lives, opening up the way to the expression of their highest potential. Paris helped Benjamin Franklin to become a great statesman: he lived there for nearly ten years, 1776–85 as the first ambassador to France for the newly declared United States, most of the time at 66 Rue Raynouard in Passy on the west side of the city, where an imposing memorial blazon on the corner of the building records he took time off to construct the first lightning conductor in France. Paris played a central part in the lives and literature of Ivan Turgenev, August Strindberg and James Joyce. Sigmund Freud's studies in Paris with Jean-Martin Charcot led him on to discover psychoanalysis, which changed forever the way we look at human nature.

Picasso came to Paris in 1900, at the age of nineteen, and a few years later settled there permanently, joining with Georges Braque to find the way into cubism, which opened the door for twentieth-century art. In Paris, Braque and Picasso did stage designs for the Russian impressario, Serge Diaghilev. Paris brought Diaghilev and Igor Stravinsky together to give birth to *The Fire Bird, Petrushka* and *The Rite of Spring.*

The early 1920s brought Man Ray to Paris from America, to set up an improvised darkroom in a lavishly decorated block of studios at 31 Rue Campagne-Première off the Boulevard du Montparnasse, where his ideas and startling originality influenced generations of photographers. Man Ray's freedom from anyone else's rules was summed up in the unmistakable syntax of another 'American in Paris', Gertrude Stein, the experimental writer who had been living there since the early 1900s: 'Man Ray is Man Ray is Man Ray is Man Ray.' she wrote. Paris made Man Ray even more Man Ray.

About a year after Man Ray arrived, Ernest Hemingway found his way over, leaving behind Toronto where he had been working as a reporter, to find in Paris a worldliness and a literary life that suited him perfectly. *A Farewell to Arms, Death in the Afternoon, For Whom the Bell Tolls* and the Nobel Prize for Literature were among the fruits.

But Paris was a very old city and we were young and nothing was simple there, not even poverty, nor sudden money, nor the

moonlight, nor right and wrong, nor the breathing of someone who lay beside you in the moonlight.
Ernest Hemingway, *A Moveable Feast*

But so far we have just browsed through a few random pages, hardly scratching the surface of what Paris has inspired and generated to add illumination, colour and delight to life on this planet. The street names in Paris will tell you more. Paris has always felt honoured by the gifted men and women who have shared and added to the life of the city and the *plaques bleues* at street corners pay homage to some of them: Place Pablo Picasso, Rue Franklin, Place Diaghilev, Place Igor Stravinsky, Avenue Marcel-Proust, Place Édith-Piaf, Square Mozart, Square Charles Dickens . . .

People not only go to Paris, they remain there. They don't just stay in hotels, they live and work in them, and die in them too sometimes. The plain stone tablet outside the Hôtel du Quai Voltaire, whose tall French windows have such a fine view over the Seine and the Tuileries Gardens, tells us it has housed Baudelaire, Sibelius, Wagner and Oscar Wilde. In fact Wagner finished writing *The Mastersingers* there. Jean-Paul Sartre lodged at the Louisiane at 60 Rue de Seine on the Left Bank, hanging his bicycle from a hook in the ceiling of his room. In 1900, 'dying beyond his means', as he characteristically quipped, Oscar Wilde died at 13 Rue des Beaux-Arts, then the simple Hôtel d'Alsace but transformed in 1968 into a four-star luxury hotel blandly called *L'Hôtel*, and charging prices that take Oscar Wilde's joke seriously.

As we might expect of them once they had made good, Scott Fitzgerald and Ernest Hemingway set themselves up at the Ritz, in the most stylish square in Paris, the Place Vendôme, a superb gallery showing off the proportion and graciousness of French seventeenth-century architecture, the most urbane out-of-doors drawing-room in the world. But instead of a plaque, the Ritz has a *Hemingway Bar*, an attraction for American tourists rich enough to be unconcerned as the impassive waiters unobtrusively keep topping up their glasses of champagne.

The bar at the Ritz is not for most writers and artists coming to Paris at the beginning of their careers. For them the pressure has always been to find cheap lodgings and even cheaper meals.

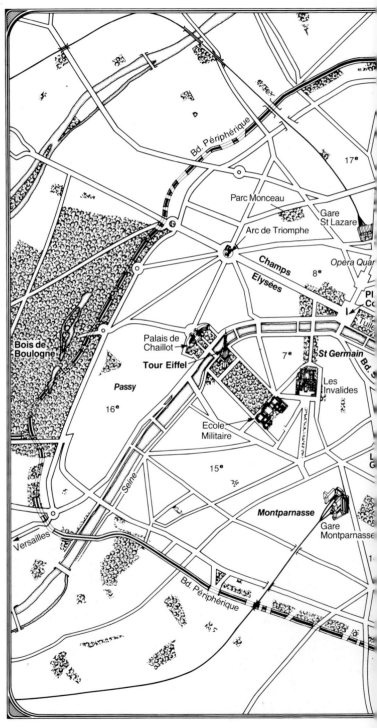

Bd. Périphérique

17e

Parc Monceau

Gare
St Lazare

Arc de Triomphe

Champs

Elysées

8e

Opéra Quar

Pl
Co

Tule

Bois de
Boulogne

Palais de
Chaillot

7e

St Germain

Bd. S

Tour Eiffel

Les
Invalides

Passy

16e

Ecole
Militaire

15e

L
G

Montparnasse

Gare
Montparnasse

Versailles

Seine

Bd. Périphérique

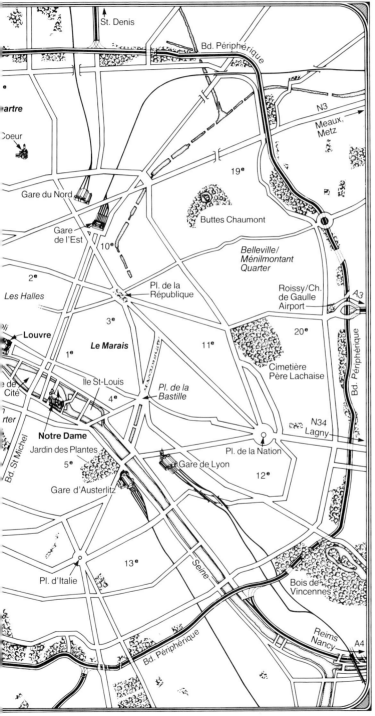

St. Denis

Bd. Périphérique

N3

Meaux,
Metz

...artre

...Coeur

19^e

Gare du Nord

Buttes Chaumont

Gare
de l'Est

10^e

Belleville/
Ménilmontant
Quarter

2^e

Pl. de la
République

Les Halles

Roissy/Ch.
de Gaulle
Airport

A3

3^e

...li

Louvre

Le Marais

11^e

20^e

1^e

Cimetière
Père Lachaise

Île St-Louis

...de
Cité

4^e

*Pl. de la
Bastille*

Bd. Périphérique

...rter

Notre Dame

N34
Lagny

Bd. St Michel

Jardin des Plantes

Pl. de la Nation

5^e

Gare de Lyon

12^e

Gare d'Austerlitz

13^e

Seine

Pl. d'Italie

Bois de
Vincennes

Reims
Nancy

A4

Bd. Périphérique

An enlightened foundation, the International City of Arts, has recognised that Paris has enriched the lives and imagination of talented people from many other countries. Since the mid-1960s, a long concrete building, looking like a dull office-block from the outside, but beautifully sited overlooking the Seine, between the Pont Louis-Philippe and the Pont Marie, makes available, for periods up to two years, studios and accommodation for writers, sculptors, painters, architects, composers, film makers, dancers and choreographers from anywhere in the world. All they pay is a portion of the actual costs of heating, laundry and maintenance. The *Cité des Arts* has already made it possible for 2,500 men and women from more than seventy different nations to draw on the creative stimulus of living in Paris, without suffering the traditional hardship and loneliness of 'starving in·a garret'.

A hotel is not a home, no matter how long you stay there. Strangers in a city, living in cramped lodgings need to get out and sit somewhere else. Writers and artists often lead lonely lives. In Paris they go to cafés to talk, to meet friends, to see and be seen. The pavements of the boulevards are wide, so cafés can spread their wicker-backed chairs and round marble-topped tables (more likely to be simulated marble these days) right out into the streets of Paris, which makes them seem more accessible, more convivial perhaps than in other cities. The cafés of Paris have long been rendezvous for writers, philosophers and revolutionaries, meeting places for literary discussion, intellectual ferment and revolutionary ideas; up to not so long ago, you could ask the waiter at some cafés to bring you pen and paper. Jean-Paul Sartre and Simone de Beauvoir more or less moved in at the Café de Flore in the Boulevard Saint-Germain. 'We worked from 9am till mid-day, when we went to lunch.' Sartre recalled, 'At two o'clock we returned and talked with our friends till four, when we resumed work until eight. After dinner, people would come to see us by appointment. All this may seem strange, but the Flore was like home to us; even when the air-raid sirens went we would pretend to leave, but instead would go up to the first floor to continue working.'

La Rotonde in the Boulevard du Montparnasse, no great distance from the Café de Flore, is a spacious restaurant now but it used to be a modest enough café. Here Lenin and Trotsky, as exiles before World War I, would take coffee together and plan the next move to bring the Bolsheviks to power. About the same time in the same café, Modigliani and Utrillo would try to drink each other under the table. It is a standing tradition in Paris cafés that customers can linger as long as they like over a coffee or a glass of wine and while it is true that a coffee at a table is not cheap any more, you can for the same price stay on as long as you like, writing your novel, meeting friends or just communing with Paris. I have never outstayed my welcome at any café table in Paris, until closing time that is, and usually that is quite late.

What is there about Paris that makes it the 'essential city', where so many new ideas in thought and art have bubbled to the surface, where according to the poet Paul Valéry, communication is more intense, more charged with meaning than anywhere else in the world? I put that question to Dr Samuel Last, a Rumanian psychiatrist who went to Paris in the 1920s to continue his medical studies, and (like Bozidar Kantuser) met his future wife there, Sonia, a beautiful Russian pianist. Sammy, as his friends call him, seemed mildly surprised by my question. *But haven't you been there?* he asked. For the moment, there was nothing more to say.

This is not to belittle London, New York, Rome, Berlin, Sydney, Tel Aviv, Tokyo and all the other great cities of the world; but there is something about the strategic setting of Paris and its confident assured reflection of the values of western civilisation that makes it call out to us in a unique way.

It is possible to love London, just as you can alternate between love and hate for the raw restless energy of New York. But with Paris it is different: if the chemistry of the place is right for you, you fall in love with it, losing your head and your heart. London is reliable, steady, sure-footed, a city for friendships formed over years in cosy pubs or in the comfortable propriety of gentlemen's clubs. New York is unstable, dynamic, with stupefying excesses, a city of instant but inconsequential intimacies. In contrast to both, Paris is insouciant, volatile, light of step, a city for endearing if not enduring love-affairs.

Its very name, when spoken by Parisians, had a fugitive lightness, as if it had been waiting for centuries for Francis Poulenc to set it to music. A true Parisian brought out the first syllable with a quick sudden tap, leaving the rest to make an arrowy flight upward. How solid and stolid was the sound of London *by comparison!*

John Russell, *Paris*

Edward Lockspeiser maintained that the guiding principle in French civilisation is 'the pleasure principle' and nowhere in France is that principle applied with more effect than in Paris. Where else would a famous restaurant have named a dessert after one of the greatest operatic sopranos of her time? When Maxims arranged peaches on vanilla ice-cream, covered it with raspberry purée and called it *Pêche Melba* in honour of one of their regular guests, they perpetuated Dame Nellie's name for generations who have never heard her sing. Where else could sex and gastronomy be so blatantly combined as in an hors-d'oeuvre poetically called *nymphes à l'aurore* ('virgins at day-break' you might say)? Nor is the recipe an anticlimax: frogs legs poached in white wine, then covered in a gently warmed sauce, served on aspic jelly and sprinkled with tarragon.

Paris even seems to have invented the whole concept of a *restaurant*. Sometime in the mid-eighteenth century, in a long-since vanished street near the fashionable Rue du Faubourg Saint-Honoré, Monsieur Boulanger started serving soup and a few dishes on marble-topped tables. Madame Boulanger who, we are told, was pretty and very appealing provided an extra attraction. As you would expect, there was no shortage of customers. M. Boulanger became the first *restaurateur*, the story goes on, since the Latin text on the sign outside his new estab-lishment promised *ego vos restaurabo*.

The original of countless *Grand Hotels* was built in Paris, in 1857 over the Café de la Paix in the Boulevard des Capucines, a well-chosen site as it turned out, because fifteen years later it overlooked the new Opéra, finished in 1872. It was in Paris that long thin sections of potato first sizzled in boiling oil and came out as *frites*, soon to become ubiquitous as *chips*. And inevitably it was in Paris that the 'French kiss' was at least defined, if not actually first tried out.

Paris remains my idea of what a city should be: where a civilised man can partake of civilised pleasures in a civilised manner and in a civilised city. **Sam White** in *The Observer*

But Paris cannot be written off as 'a stately pleasure-dome', even though it can seem like that at times. There is also a serious purposefulness in the air, which has spurred people on to greater personal achievements in whatever field they are working. The nineteenth-century writer and historian, Joseph Renon, is said to have reproached a student from Oxford for having the wrong idea. 'You Englishmen think of Paris as a great fairground,' he said, 'a place of fun and games. I tell you it is nothing of the sort. It is the hardest working place in the world.' James Joyce, who settled in Paris after World War I, had the same experience. 'There is an atmosphere of spiritual effort here,' he wrote to a friend in 1921, 'No other city is quite like it. It is a racehorse tension. I wake early, often at five o'clock, and start writing at once.'

Perhaps it is this peculiarly poised balance between sensuous pleasures and the most stringent intellectual and creative effort that gives Paris its special quality. As far back as the thirteenth century, the University of Paris was already the intellectual centre of the western world. Ever since, Paris has been a city where ideas are in a constant state of ebullition, where one movement follows another, not only in art and fashion, but in the very texture of thought itself. This is still partly linked with the Sorbonne, founded in 1257 by Robert de Sorbon, chaplain and confessor to Louis IX. The Sorbonne has a different relationship with Paris than any other university in a capital city. In Great Britain, the ancient universities of Oxford and Cambridge take clear precedence over the University of London, which was not founded until the nineteenth century. Harvard and Yale have more prestige than the universities in Washington and New York. But the Sorbonne (which is really only part of the University of Paris) is the true centre of higher learning in France.

Not that the dreary buildings of the Sorbonne, all nineteenth century except the chapel, have any special distinction. The main courtyard, the Cour d'Honneur, functionally paved to take the steady traffic of students criss-crossing it to get to lecture halls, has none of the dignity and verdant peace of Oxford and Cambridge quadrangles. The small Place de la Sorbonne, now a university precinct, does have a warmer more intimate quality, with cafés all around and a pleasant open space

Place de la Sorbonne

where students can meet and talk. The façade of the Chapel of the Sorbonne, on the east side of the *place*, dominates it, providing a sense of history and tradition. The chapel, and when it was finished in 1642 it was seen to be as big as a church, is all that remains of Richelieu's rebuilding of the Sorbonne. The triumphant dome, as high as the church is long, heralds the other domes you see on the skyline of Paris, such as the domes of the Panthéon and Les Invalides.

The chapel is used now for exhibitions rather than for services (the official university church is Saint-Séverin on the other side of the Boulevard Saint-Germain), except it seems for one mass a year for the soul of Richelieu. Paris has a fancy for relics and the ceremonial red hat of Cardinal Richelieu hangs from the ceiling of the church, just as, in a different context, Primo Carnera's boxing gloves hang from the ceiling of Harry's Bar near the Opéra.

It is not the architecture that distinguishes the Sorbonne but its reputation as one of the most formidable 'think-tanks' in the world, the sharpest focus of intellectual energy, in the tradition of teachers such as Joseph Renon, Claude Lévi-Strauss and Jean-Paul Sartre.

When you are in Paris, passing so many private art galleries in the Marais, and along the quays and up towards Saint-Germain-des-Prés, looking at the array of so many colourful posters advertising art exhibitions, constantly being replaced, the way cut flowers are, in so many bars and cafés, visiting the audacious breathtaking new Musée d'Orsay, enjoying the quiet of the intimate personal Picasso Museum, opened in 1985, it is easy to accept the self-confident stance that Paris adopts, as naturally the first city in the world for art. It is as if every other place, despite evidence to the contrary, is merely derivative. Paris became the undisputed centre of art in the nineteenth century, in the way that Rome had been in the seventeenth century and Florence in the fifteenth. For the history of nineteenth-century painting in Europe is mostly the story of breaking away from conventions, exploring new directions. The stage where this was being acted out was the art world of Paris.

Paris, of course, personified and located the idea of *la vie bohème*, artists living free untrammelled lives, disdainful of the cares and responsibilities that inhibit most of us. The

Montmartre of Utrillo, Modigliani, Dufy, Picasso, Braque can never be relived, but the narrow cobbled streets and old houses are still there, and the legends linger on. Early in the twentieth century the art scene shifted to Montparnasse, bringing with it Chagall, Léger, Matisse, Picasso and Braque, a parade of names that made the Montparnasse district of Paris the starting point of modern art in the twentieth century.

Most of the art 'isms' started in Paris, including two fundamental turning-points in the whole history of western art, impressionism and cubism. Between them came fauvism, also in Paris. While dadaism had its origins in Zurich, it was in Paris, in the years just after World War I, that it was used as the springboard for the artistic exploration of the subconscious, looking at people and things in an altogether new way. This was the movement that led on to surrealism.

Revolution and change are never far away for long in Paris. The French Revolution, which of course began in Paris with the storming of the Bastille on the 14th July 1789, remains the most revolutionary of revolutions, not only in the history of France but of the world. It was dominated by Paris where an outspoken press, powerful orators and the tradition of mob power on the streets combined to build up the momentum to carry it through. When the barricades went up again in 1848, Paris was dominant once more, forcing changes on the whole of France, as the new provisional government declared that every man had the right to vote, at a time when universal suffrage existed nowhere else in Europe. 17–18 March 1871 was another night of the barricades, and some historians see that as the first worker uprising in the history of the world, with the communards, the members of the new Paris Commune, carrying out an early experiment in Marxist socialism.

Nearly a hundred years later, in May 1968, the Sorbonne and the *Beaux-Arts* were on the streets, with the students proclaiming *Il est interdit d'interdire* (it is forbidden to forbid). Student posters appeared all over Paris, some of which have now become valuable collectors' items. Once again Paris led the whole of France, as the violent pitched battles in the Latin Quarter between students and police brought out on strike more than nine million people, the unions losing control of their members and the government in disarray.

École des Beaux-Arts

Paris never loses its revolutionary potential and Parisians seem as ready as ever to go out protesting on to the streets, not in the quiet banner-carrying processions you sometimes see in London, with unarmed police patiently walking alongside, but as an angry mob, with garrisons of riot police, the heavily armed *CRS*, marshalled at strategic points. It is ironic that although the authorities are quick to take action at the first hint of insurgence, the *quatorze juillet* remains the most important festival in the French calendar. It is a public holiday, of course, long tricolours flutter from both sides of every lamp-post along the two miles of the Champs-Élysées, from the Place de la Concorde to the Arc de Triomphe, fire-crackers are set off all over Paris and there is dancing in the streets.

In 1981 President Mitterrand launched a whole series of *Grands Projets*, to 'help us to understand our roots and our history' he said, as part of a colossal celebration in permanent form of the bicentenary in 1989 of the French Revolution. Mitterrand is the latest in a line of men in power who have the loftiest ambitions to make Paris pre-eminent among the cities of the world. When Napoleon Bonaparte was sailing towards Egypt in 1798, he was already planning, if he became master of France, to make Paris 'not only the most beautiful city in being but the most beautiful which had ever been or ever would be.' With some glaring exceptions maybe, such ambitions have been well served by architects, even in everyday matters like the original art nouveau entrances to Métro stations, with tall willowy cast-iron lamps like the amber flowers of some exotic plant. These still survive at some stations such as the Louvre, Bastille, Cité, Abbesses in Montmartre and the Métro by the Parc de Monceau. This is living functional open-air art in Paris, designed in 1900 by Hector Guimard, including his leaf-life art nouveau nameblock, *METROPOLITAN*. When the entrance to the Métro Raspail was replaced, the original was snapped up by the sculpture section of the Metropolitan Museum of Modern Art in New York.

In the 1980s Paris will have spent nearly a thousand million pounds on five major museum projects. The Parisian passion during this time, for combining building on the grand scale with looking ahead to the twenty-first century, stakes out a claim for Paris to be considered the architectural capital of modern

Europe and the most truly civilised city in the world.

President Mitterrand and Colbert would have understood each other – they both inspired new hope for the city – not just for Paris but for the civilised world.
Financial Times, 11 April 1987

When Kenneth Clark in the 1960s wrote and narrated his famous television series called *Civilisation*, where did he begin the very first programme? It was in Paris, standing on the Pont des Arts.

Paris is a concentrated city. London, for example, has no obvious limits: you never know where the city begins or ends as it sprawls untidily and endlessly in all directions. But as Manhattan is an island, bounded by the Hudson River and the East River, Paris is also contained, beginning and ending as it has done for a long time at the gates: the Porte d'Orléans, Porte d'Italie, Porte de Versailles and the others. Beyond the gates are the *banlieues*, the outskirts. So for all the changes that have taken place, Paris remains extraordinarily *Paris*.

Nobody can love Paris *all* the time. Or can they? Traffic can be horrendous and to be imprisoned on a hot day, in the midst of a crawling mass of pulsating metal and a pollution of fumes, is like a nightmare. Paris drivers can be more selfish and impatient than most (France has the highest number of road accidents of any country in Europe), pedestrian crossings are a joke, parking like cramming yet another book into an already full bookshelf, *police-secours* sirens are forever startling the air, treks through Métro stations to change trains seem interminable (although Métros are usually immaculate and efficient), and the bored officiousness in post offices is frustrating. Even in the early nineteenth century, long before the traffic jams, Hazlitt, the English essayist, found Paris 'a beast of a city to be in'. But for most of us Paris soon becomes life-enhancing again, instead of life-destroying, and all is forgiven, the way we forgive faults in someone we love.

Other great capital cities have their admirers, but Paris has lovers who cannot even bear to be separated from her for a single day. Mercier, who lived in the reign of Louis XVI, was so fond of Paris that he declared he would rather live in prison there than in freedom elsewhere.

Harold P. Clunn, *The Face of Paris*

When the spell is binding, Paris is a charmer. Although the climate is not all that different from London, Paris puts on a show of being a Mediterranean city, open and free, cafés spreading out into the streets, couples kissing and embracing anywhere, anytime. And it is the most sensuous of cities, where giving pleasure has become an art, eating is calculated self-indulgence and even the humblest of bars parade a dazzling array of brandies, whiskies and apéritifs. Window-dressing in the Rue Faubourg St-Honoré is so much more than displaying goods for sale: it is décor, design, wit and above all *style*, a word that seems more at home in the French language, where it first belonged.

Of course Paris did not invent sex and passion, although sometimes you might think it did, as encounters there between men and women seem to be sharper and more intense, with sexual tension hovering in the air like heat haze. A love-affair in Paris has a volatile flavour all of its own. Thomas Carlyle captured it in his description of Voltaire's relationship with Madame de Châtelet . . . 'This literary amour wears but a mixed aspect: short sungleams with tropical showers, touches of guitar music soon followed by Lisbon earthquakes . . .' Parisiennes are usually well aware of their femininity, or at least of their sexuality, and there is nothing reticent about the way men look at attractive women, or the other way round.

At every turn in Paris there is a generous outpouring of energy just go give pleasure. As you walk along the streets, the sweet smells wafting from the seductive displays of pastries in the *pâtisseries*, the piquant aromas from the smoked meats and sausages in the *charcuteries*, the bewildering choice of cheeses in the *fromageries* (you can have a different French cheese for every day of the year), the fragrances coming from the flower shops and the *parfumeries*, the jazz groups playing on Sunday mornings under arcades in the Place des Vosges, never let us forget for long that, whatever other reason brings us to Paris, we are also here to enjoy ourselves.

'I haven't been to Paris for years', people say to you. But nearly

*everyone has a formative memory that is connected with the place –
of a lost virginity, of a lost wallet, or one or other of the experiences
which we are all supposed to carry with us through life.*

Frank Johnson, former Paris correspondent of *The Times*

To get the most out of Paris you have to leave behind London,
New York, Manchester, Seattle, Adelaide or wherever, and become a little bit Parisian yourself, no matter how scrappy your
French is. For that reason, *Paris: The Essential City* is not a
guide book, limited to prices, dates and facts. It is written to
help you tune into the heartbeat and pulse-rate of this beautiful
and incredibly rewarding city, to encourage you to become part
of it, going just a little further than you think you can dare. Then
you will be able to sit down with a coffee, croissants and brioches
in front of you, at a table on the terrace of *Aux Deux Magots*, the
former 'existentialist' café in Saint-Germain-des-Prés, where at
one time your bill was stamped *Le Rendez-vous de l'élite intellec-
tuelle*, give a deep sigh of pleasure, and feel at last – *enfin!* – you
are here in Paris.

Note: Sterling and US dollar equivalents throughout this book
are based on an exchange rate of £1 to $1.65. Where
equivalents for French francs are mentioned, the rate taken is
ten francs to £1 or six francs to $1.

ART AND ARTISTS

Perhaps it was François I, with his passion for the Italian Renaissance, who took the first step towards making Paris the world centre of art. He became King in 1515 when he was only twenty and that same year invaded Italy. As well as winning a glorious victory at Marignano, SE of Milan, François sought out Leonardo da Vinci and invited him to come to France. He came the following year; and there in France for the remaining few years of his life was the most complete genius of the Renaissance, lodged at the pleasant manor house of Clos-Lucé in Amboise, by the Loire Valley. Leonardo brought with him the portrait he had painted in Florence of 'Mona Lisa', which the King purchased for his own collection, and which hangs, protected by bomb-proof concrete and bullet-proof glass, in the *Salle des États* of the Louvre, where every day, except Tuesdays and public holidays, a procession slowly shuffles past it as an obligatory ritual, part of everyone's first visit to Paris.

Partly because the 'Mona Lisa' hangs there, *Collection de François 1ier* neatly noted beneath it, the Louvre is maybe the most famous museum in the world. It is certainly the most solemn and the most oppressive. But there is a new *Grand Projet* afoot, a total replanning of the whole museum, that is intended to change all that.

The Louvre sits as massive . . . as the British Museum and
National Gallery rolled into one and more besides. It presents at
once a duty and a temptation; an indigestible confusion of riches
and the prospect of inordinate pleasure.
William Packer, *Financial Times*

The Louvre started out as a fortress, built by King Philippe Auguste between 1190 and 1200 to protect Paris from invasion from downstream. François I wanted to rebuild it as his palace on the lines of the *palazzos* he had seen and admired in Italy, and in 1546 work started on the new Palais du Louvre. François died the following year but work continued, in many ways still following his wishes, which is why the façades in the *Cour Carrée* have a classical Italianate look about them; the façade designed by Pierre Lescot, whom François had commissioned, has been described as the most masterly demonstration of French classical architecture. The story of the Louvre after that is one of continual aggrandizement by successive rulers until by the end of the nineteenth century it almost dominated the centre of Paris. Nathaniel Hawthorne, the American novelist, was overwhelmed when he saw it. 'I never knew what a palace was,' he wrote, 'until I had a glimpse of the Louvre.'

It was only in 1793, a few years after the Revolution, that for the first time part of the great palace, the Grande Gallerie, was opened as a museum. And just in time too, for not so long after that loot from Napoleon's conquests came pouring in, from Florence, from Venice, from Bologna, from Vienna, from Antwerp, from The Hague, from anywhere where Napoleon had conquered and the artistic pickings were good. The ground floor of the Louvre was in chaos, paintings and sculpture still in their packing-cases. Later many of these treasures were returned, including the four magnificent golden-bronze horses of Nero, taken from St Marks in Venice (which had in turn looted them in the thirteenth century from Constantinople as it then was) which Napoleon had ordered to be hoisted aloft on top of the Arc de Triomphe du Carrousel, where they remained for sixteen years, 1809–25 looking straight up the Champs-Élysées. But a lot of paintings and sculpture remained in the Louvre enriching still further the collection. The first masterpiece in residence is the one that is easiest to find, because from the moment you enter, there are signs pointing the way towards the 'Mona Lisa'. Many visitors resolutely follow those signs, hardly looking to the right or the left, as they pass through fabulous salons and drawing-rooms, the almost endless *Grande Galerie* hung with masterpieces of French art from the seventeenth and eighteenth centuries, through the Medici Gallery, full of

Rubens' great canvases devoted entirely to Marie de Medici, Queen and Regent of France. On they go, following the signs until at last they reach the *Salle des États*, a much less impressive room. There they find a chattering crowd, not unlike a cocktail party, except that people have cameras in their hands instead of glasses. Pushing their way through they stand in front of Leonardo da Vinci's famous painting, very likely for the first and only time, not quite knowing what to think or to say. No work of art has ever had such demands made upon it.

Walter Pater, the Victorian art critic, thought the 'Mona Lisa' was literally out of this world: 'She is older than the rocks among which she sits.' he wrote, 'Like the vampire, she has been dead many times, and learned the secrets of the grave . . . and, as Leda, was the mother of Helen of Troy, and, as Saint Anne, the mother of Mary . . .' A few years later the French painter, Marcel Duchamp, one of the leaders of the dada movement in New York, protested against such hyperbole by painting a copy of Leonardo's picture, correct in every detail, but adding a moustache to the celebrated enigmatic smile. More recently, in 1987 in *The Guardian*, a writer described the portrait as 'an insanely overrated picture'. Yet to go to Paris without seeing the 'Mona Lisa' at least once would be like going to Agra without seeing the Taj Mahal.

A few feet away in the Louvre, to the left of where the 'Mona Lisa' hangs, away from the crowds and the cameras, you can stand alone looking at what is arguably a greater, infinitely more tender and more profound Leonardo, the 'Madonna and Child with Saint Anne'. This is a divinely proportioned grouping with that mysterious balance between languor and intensity characteristic of Leonardo at his greatest. 'What searchings must he not have gone through,' Bernard Berenson wrote about it, 'before he attained to . . . the exquisite balance of masses, the harmonious rhythm of expression rippling from face to face . . .'

Of course there are many other treasures in the Louvre. Rodin used to say that a visit there affected him like beautiful music or a deep emotion. Henry James found the Gallery of Apollo, which you enter through beautiful seventeenth-century wrought-iron gates, 'the world in fine raised to the richest and noblest expression'. And few things are as stirring as experiencing for the first time that dynamic thrust forward against the wind of the 'Winged Victory of Samothrace', which at the top of a wide flight of stairs is possibly the most perfectly sited work of art in the whole vast museum.

It is too soon to say whether President Mitterrand's bold plan, declared in 1981, will transform the Louvre from a cavernous echoing mausoleum of masterpieces into a place where we can move round and enjoy great art in a living welcoming environment. Part of the Ministry of Finance, which occupied one-third of the palace, has been moved out into a new building in the suburbs, to create more space for exhibits, and a Chinese-American architect, Ieoh Ming Pei, was chosen to design a huge new 'pyramid' in the centre of the Cour Napoléon, the main palace courtyard, as a new reception area, to welcome the Louvre's three million visitors a year. It is daring and controversial to build something so uncompromisingly modern in such a famous historic setting and there is much criticism of what is going on. 'However,' the prospectus boldly maintains, 'contemporary creativity cannot be stifled by a passive respect for one's heritage. Ancient and modern, that is to say, timeless, the pyramid will animate its environment without challenging it.' It is too early to judge, or even to know for certain how much of the total plan for the Louvre will be carried out, although, we can admire the grand concept and the courage to take risks.

Although there is a marvellous collection of art at the Louvre, it is not for great classical and Renaissance paintings and sculpture that Paris is, in most people's minds, the City of Art. The collections at the Uffizi in Florence, at the Accademia in Venice are also legendary. But Paris alone is the city of Delacroix, Renoir, Manet, Monet, Rodin, Picasso, Braque, Chagall, Léger, Matisse, Soutine and of so many other artists who have given expression to the major movements of the nineteenth and twentieth centuries that have dominated art in the whole of the western world.

The history of art in Paris since the early nineteenth century follows the social and political history of France after the Revolution, with one new concept following another, each one breaking up more of the traditional mould which kept academic art formalised and inflexible. Eugène Delacroix, early on in the nineteenth century, started the first new trend, dismissing imitation of Greek and Roman art and making colour more important than clarity of outline. This prepared the ground for the movements that followed. As the century unfolded, François Millet and Gustave Courbet opened the way to acceptance of everyday scenes and ordinary people as fitting subjects for painting, not even excluding what would have been considered commonplace and ugly. *Le Réalisme*, Courbet called it at his exhibition in Paris in 1855, one of the first 'isms' in art history.

Édouard Manet went further in exploring how colour, light and shade actually appear to us when we look at them. He abandoned the carefully worked gradations from dark to light, as it was so precisely formulated in academic art teaching at the time. The result is we can relate so much more immediately to Manet's pictures, because they in turn relate directly to life as it appears. But at the time some of his paintings were rejected out of hand for exhibition at the official Paris Salon of 1863, as were paintings by other artists, including Whistler and Cézanne, who were also experimenting in new directions. Pressure built up for a separate exhibition to show the work of all the painters who had been refused. This was the famous *Salon des Refusés*, the first ever 'fringe' show, with Paris again taking the lead in art history.

European art in the last quarter of the nineteenth century was again focussed on Paris, with one movement dominating the scene, *impressionism*, an attractive poetic word, possibly the most well known of all art 'isms', just as impressionist paintings are perhaps the most immediately enjoyable. The word is used loosely, often rather vaguely, because how could artists as gifted as Monet, Renoir, Sisley, Camille Pissarro, Cézanne, although undoubtedly with a distinctive approach in common, not give precedence to their own style and individuality? You can recognise their pictures as *impressionist* but you usually know at once which artist painted it.

The impressionists cared less for detail than for capturing the spontaneous effect, putting down what they saw straight on to the canvas without pondering. Monet believed that painting must be done on the spot, instead of taking sketches back to the studio to work on, catching momentary changes in light, which is why he sometimes painted the same subject at different times of the day. 'Light', he said, 'is the chief personage in a picture'. Critics were outraged at what seemed to them irresponsible slapdash art and the Paris Salon of 1873 threw out the pictures of the entire group. So they held their own show, at the photographic studio of Nadar, an outstanding pioneer in portrait photography, at 35 Boulevard des Capucines, between the Madeleine and the Opéra. Unexpectedly no memorial tablet marks the place where the first impressionist exhibition was held, although it is such a turning-point in the history of art. There is a restaurant on the first floor of the building called *Les Impressionistes* but how many people eating there pick up the allusion?

Impressionism, a name taken, derisively to begin with, from the title of a painting by Monet which he called 'Impression – Sunrise', freed painters to communicate more directly their own personal vision. It became the most talked about art movement in the world, attracting artists from everywhere to work and study in Paris, to enjoy freedom from conventions and preconceived ideas. Not that many art critics at the time saw it that way. *Le Figaro* wrote '. . . five or six lunatics, one of them a woman, a group of unfortunates corrupted by the folly of ambition, have met here to exhibit their works . . . What a horrible spectacle this is of human conceit stretched to the edge of dementia.' The woman was Berthe Morisot, who had been a pupil of Manet. The other 'lunatics' were Renoir, Pissarro, Cézanne and Monet! As always the shouting and passions of the past become history in the present. In December 1986 all Paris was complaining about the enormous queues to get in to see paintings by the artists, who were so violently abused in the 1870s and thrown out by the establishment, hung in a sensational new museum, the *Musée d'Orsay*, across the Seine, a little way downstream from the Louvre.

The Gare d'Orsay, a grandiose glass-roofed arched railway station, grander than Grand Central Station, was completed in 1900 in time for the great Universal Exhibition in Paris. This old station, which had become a disused white elephant, dilapidated and ghostly, just the setting for a film director with the macabre imagination of Orson Welles, who chose it to shoot some scenes for his film version of Kafka's *The Trial*, has been converted into a spectacular museum.

A visitor from the past, standing on the other side of the river, would still see the familiar railway station, the original baroque station clock in place and telling the right time, everything

Place du Tertre in Montmartre

seemingly unchanged, except that it has been cleaned up. Even as you go through the entrance, the feeling of a railway station persists, with people hesitantly looking for their platforms, the iron girders still bolted together. But a few steps on, you see that the great concourse, from which trains used to arrive and depart, has become a magnificent temple of the visual arts, a glorious celebration of life on earth, with arresting grandeur and spaciousness. Inevitably some critics have found fault with one aspect or another but the sheer presumption, the brilliance of the adaptation of one of the most valuable sites in Europe, if not in the world, into a stupendous art museum, leaves you breathless. The Musée d'Orsay was instant greatness, and so confident was it of immediate world fame, that right from the opening day it abbreviated itself as the *M'O*.

Now, once more queues are forming, this time to savour the fulfilment of a 19th century Parisian dream. Paris is herself again: Paris the world capital in the Musée d'Orsay!
William Feaver in *The Observer*

The plan of the Musée d'Orsay is simple, the intentions more complex. It is a museum of art, in its widest aspects, of the second half of the nineteenth century. The precisely chosen period is between 1850, the beginning of Corbet's realism, when nineteenth-century French art was taking new directions, and around 1905, just before the birth of cubism, which was the beginning of twentieth-century art. The intention of the museum, as stated, is to be 'the gathering point for the art of an era' with all artistic forms included: painting, sculpture, architecture, the decorative arts, photography, posters and even film production. The attempt is to integrate all these expressions, so you might turn at one moment from a painting to a piece of sculpture to a piece of furniture.

In practice, until we get used to the impact of the place and are able to relate to its programme, most visitors are likely to go there as much for the building itself and for the delightful view across Paris to the Sacré-Coeur, looking through the hands of the giant station clock, as for the collections of art. They will of course look at the sculpture on the ground floor, taking in some of the epic academic paintings, which some critics complain

The Pompidou Centre – 'that inside-out place'

have been given pride of place. Then they may walk through the side gallery given over to aspects of realism, stopping irresistibly in front of Manet's 'Déjeuner sur l'herbe' ('picnic on the grass' you could say) one of the most famous paintings of the nineteenth century. Manet's painting of a nubile young woman stark naked, calmly having a picnic with two elegantly dressed gentlemen, was shown in 1863 at the 'fringe' Salon in Paris. It caused such a scandal that it led to the early closing of the whole exhibition, and became the challenging manifesto for the new generation of painters.

After that most visitors will make a bee-line for the escalators or the lift going to the upper level, to look at the most celebrated paintings in the whole museum, the greatest collection of impressionist art in the world. Others may walk up instead, and the extra effort will be rewarded because the stairs take them past the whirls and sinuous twists of art nouveau furniture and designs, including one of Hector Guimard's original Métro entrances. The first director of the Musée d'Orsay is Françoise Cachin. She works in a white and grey office, made of metal tubes and lacquered sheet steel, and insists that the museum is an *art* museum and that furniture and designs are there not as social history or to illustrate a life style, but are chosen because of their aesthetic quality.

When at last you reach the upper level, you will share Monet's love-affair with colour and light in his 'Autumn Haystack', or his studies of a woman with a parasol, painted twice to catch variations of light, and in the fleeting effects of reflections on the surface of water in his garden at Giverny. On another wall is Renoir's joyous painting of the Moulin de la Galette, the dance-hall in Montmartre that was all the rage at the turn of the century. Further along is a superb group of van Goghs. Long after the novelty of the building itself has worn off, this glorious collection of impressionist and post-impressionist paintings will always make the *M'O* a place of pilgrimage.

Where the Musée d'Orsay stops, around 1905, the Pompidou Centre begins. The Centre National d'Art Contemporain Georges Pompidou, not surprisingly shortened to the *Centre Pompidou*, or known to Parisians even more simply as the *Beaubourg* (after the Rue Beaubourg where it is situated), is focussed on twentieth-century art and looking beyond, to the twenty-first century. This starts with the building itself, the most outrageously contentious art centre that has been built anywhere so far, alongside which even Frank Lloyd Wright's Guggenheim Museum on 5th Avenue, New York seems but modestly innovative.

At the outset, the brief to architects called for 'a living information centre'. The designers who won the open competition, an Italian, Renzo Piano, and an Englishman, Richard Rogers, almost unknown at the time but now one of the most talked about of all architects, delivered what was asked for: the Pompidou Centre vibrates with neoterisms, projects futurisms and uses cool confident neologisms. The building itself looks like a vast pop art intestinal tract, with bright red, blue and green pipes and ventilator shafts on the outside, as well as an exterior escalator zig-zagging its way up to the top. 'That ugly inside-out place' Parisians called it when it opened in February 1977. Opinions about it were so violently divergent that they divided families, almost broke up marriages and caused stand-up fights. But like the Eiffel Tower, the beloved symbol of Paris, which in its early days was called 'the great black factory chimney', the Pompidou Centre has become another classic *succès de scandale*. Its very notoriety attracted so much publicity that it has popularised modern art as never before, becoming the most visited museum of any kind in the world. And now exterior escalators, pipes and air-ducts have been accepted even by the conservative Lloyd's of London as a feature of their new building. Not that the Pompidou Centre cannot still come as a shock, when you round a corner into the Rue Beaubourg and see it unexpectedly, looking like a garish oil refinery in the heart of Paris, with the twin Gothic towers of Notre-Dame visible in the distance, the two worlds clashing in irreconcilable discord.

For the moment, then, the Pompidou Centre tends not to be widely acknowledged as the masterpiece it unquestionably is, for compromised as it may be by capricious fire regulations and political contingencies the finished building exudes a rare thoroughness, consistency and beauty.

Brian Appleyard, *Richard Rogers*

Zig-zagging up the Pompidou Centre

Inside there is a sense of boundless space and feverish energy, with visitors of all ages milling around not quite knowing where to turn next: 'People flick from room to room at Beaubourg,' commented John Russell, the art critic on the New York Times, 'the way they flick from channel to channel on a television set.' The crowds visibly moving up and down the glass tubes of escalators outside the building add to the feeling of continuous jittery change of perspective and even the portrait, suspended in mid-air, of the late President Georges Pompidou is Op-Art, by Vasarély, so that it always seems on the move.

The nearest to anything permanent in the Pompidou Centre is the collection in the National Museum of Modern Art on the third and fourth floors, which is one of the greatest collections in the world of twentieth-century art. Although there are painters exhibited, such as Pierre Bonnard (1867–1947), whose work spans the nineteenth and twentieth centuries, modern art at the Pompidou Centre takes off with *cubism*. This was Picasso's great adventure, which he shared with Georges Braque, encouraged by Cézanne's famous advice 'to look at nature in terms of cubes, cones and cylinders'. You can see here how the two painters were exploring in this direction, including landmarks in cubist art, such as Braque's 'Young Girl with a Guitar' and Picasso's 'Seated Woman'. Picasso went further still, pushing cubism towards abstract art. Some of his paintings at the Pompidou Centre have become so decomposed as to be almost unrecognisable. Many of the other artists, as well as Picasso, whose work is shown in the Museum of Modern Art, were not French. Kandinsky was Russian. In 1910 he painted what is regarded as the first true 'abstract', believing that painting, like music, could move into 'pure' expression. Brancusi, who settled in Paris in 1904, was Rumanian. Alexander Calder, the sculptor who invented the mobile, was American. Modigliani, who also settled in Paris as a young man, was Italian.

Most of these expatriates knew each other in Paris, where they shared ideas during the early years of the twentieth century when the frontiers of art were being pushed further and further back, with cubism anticipating abstract art, dadaism moving into surrealism. At the Pompidou Centre, the psycho-fantasies of surrealism are represented by Salvador Dali, Max Ernst and Miro. All these movements are well set out here, yet you come away more with the impact of an individual striving for self-expression. Pierre Bonnard wrote: 'I do not belong to any school but seek only to create something personal.' Matisse, who made such joyfully fresh and lively pictures by cutting out coloured paper, said that 'to cut out shapes spontaneously in colour reminds me of the direct plasticity of sculpture'. Brancusi's 'Seal' in grey and white marble is personal and tender. There are few places anywhere in the world, as on the fourth floor of the Pompidou Centre, where you feel such a direct contact with the extraordinary diversity of human response to being alive.

The restless activity inside the Pompidou Centre spills out on to the *Plateau Beaubourg*, the name given to the big cobbled area in front. It is always crowded, perhaps because of the constant side-shows offered by buskers of all kinds, perhaps because entrance to the Centre is free and you can ride up and down on the escalators as often as you like for a moving panoramic view over Paris, perhaps because the whole place is one constant 'happening', which gives people, especially young people, a feeling of being in touch with the year, the month, the day, the moment they are living through. The *Genitron*, a large computer-like contraption, now installed in front of the Centre, adds to this feeling of everything there being *here and now*, by counting down in large flashing figures the number of seconds remaining until the end of the millenium, midnight on 31 December 1999.

Art and artists are all around in Paris. In one district alone near the Boulevard Malesherbes, which leads out from the Madeleine, you could come across streets named after Rembrandt, van Dyke, Murillo, Ruysdael, and Velazquez. There is a Rue Van Gogh near the Gare de Lyon, a Rue Rubens near where Gobelin tapestries are made and a Terrasse Modigliani near the former artists' cafés in Montparnasse. Rodin, as befits the greatest French sculptor, gets both an avenue and a square named after him. Not far from the Étoile you will find the Rue Léonard-de-Vinci, and you can pass along the Avenue Ingres on the way to the Bois de Boulogne.

In the Square Laurent Prache, a quiet garden beside the church of Saint-German-des-Prés, there is a bronze by Picasso, which he dedicated to his friend, the poet Guillaume Apollinaire, one of the first to recognise cubism as an important movement in art and who later coined the word *surrealist*. The

Art Nouveau Métro Abbesses

Place des Abbesses in Montmartre has the best art nouveau Métro entrance, unchanged since it was designed by Hector Guimard about 1900. In the Rue Vieille du Temple in the Marais there is a jewel of an art nouveau café, called *Au Petit Fer à Cheval*, 'at the little horseshoe', a simple place serving drinks and cheap meals for locals, with a horseshoe-shaped marble counter and original turn of the century tiles, gilded chandelier and baroque cash-register.

A small district of Paris, on a hill to the north, was for a few years world famous for its offbeat life-style and as the centre of avant-garde art in Europe. Montmartre, 'the Mount of Martyrs' according to legend, because Christian martyrs were said to have been beheaded there, or more familiarly called, by those who want to show they are in the know, the *Butte*, the 'hillock', was a country village with windmills grinding the flour for Paris. The ramshackle houses, cheap rents and easy-going way of life attracted many artists who were coming to Paris towards the end of the nineteenth century. The Moulin-Rouge, the old 'red windmill', opened in the Place Blanche in 1889, with its saucy cabaret and cancan girls. Toulouse-Lautrec became the unofficial artist in residence, drawing singers, dancers, prostitutes and producing a series of brilliant posters, such as the ones portraying the singer Yvette Guilbert with her scarlet hair and long black gloves. These made the Moulin-Rouge and the 'café-concerts' of Montmartre the sensation of Paris.

The lights winking up at a pallid moon, the slender painted ladies, the wings of the Moulin-Rouge, the smell of petrol and perfume and cooking. The Place Blanche, Paris. Life itself.

Jean Rhys, *Quartet*

Halfway up the hill towards the top of the *Butte*, in the quiet Place Émile-Goudeau, was the Bateau-Lavoir, a dilapidated lodging-house where it is possible, if anywhere, to pinpoint the beginnings of twentieth-century art as we know it. Picasso took a room here in 1904, when he returned to Paris aged twenty-three and hard-up, and stayed on until 1912. Braque, Modigliani, van Dongen, Juan Gris, Max Jacob, Marie Laurençin and Apollinaire were among the others who moved into rooms in the building, to form an experimental circle working in new directions.

Cobbled street in Montmartre

Working here during the winter of 1906–7 most of Picasso's energy went into his monumental painting, 'Les Demoiselles d'Avignon', a violent rejection of normal perspective that was at the time altogether bewildering to Matisse and Picasso's other friends, when they saw it overwhelming his tiny atelier. Some art historians see this as the key painting in twentieth-century art, leading on to cubism, abstract art and the eventual freedom of artists to challenge the very definition of art. Yet it was not exhibited in public until thirty years later. 'Les Demoiselles d'Avignon' is now in the Museum of Modern Art in New York but you can see some of the preliminary studies for it in Paris, in the Picasso Museum.

Just as it was about to be turned into a museum in 1970, the Bateau-Lavoir was sadly destroyed by fire. So there is not much to see there now except the new artist's studios that have been built, although you can sit on one of the benches in the pleasant leafy Place Émile-Goudeau and reflect on how much this gentle corner of Montmartre has contributed to modern art.

Higher up, now at the top of the *Butte*, is another square, neither quiet nor gentle but usually crowded with tourists day and night, packed with cafés and art shops, making what they can of the legend of Montmartre, as the place where great artists painted masterpieces, drank heavily, went hungry and followed the free-living bohemian way of life set to music by Puccini in *La Bohème*. The Place du Tertre, behind the Sacré-Coeur, is still a powerful attraction for tourists, looking for something they will never find, the Montmartre of Picasso, Modigliani and others, long since gone. But people come here just the same to buy paintings 'in genuine oil paint', done by artists who at least look the part with beards and corduroys, or to have their own portraits drawn or painted. Many of them pay £100 (about $165) or much more, with a vague feeling, altogether illusory of course, that Picasso or Utrillo or van Gogh have somehow been involved. Yet if they were to walk only a little way off, to the quiet cobbled Rue Cortot, away from the kitsch and the clamour, they would be so much closer to the real feeling of Montmartre as it was, when Renoir, van Gogh, Dufy, Utrillo and the others lived and worked nearby.

12 Rue Cortot has been turned into the Museum of Montmartre, inconsequential as museums go and not much

Utrillo's studio in Montmartre

visited, but with a certain charm. It contains, among other relics, the well-worn zinc bar from Monsieur Baillot's old café, and is worth visiting just to sit in the simple peaceful garden, looking up at Maurice Utrillo's studio with its big 'north light' window, where, drinking his way through all the absinthe and wine he could get hold of, he worked on his familiar paintings, which have such perfect beauty of composition, of the narrow streets and tumbledown houses of Montmartre.

Even before World War I, the art scene in Paris was showing signs of shifting to the other side of the Seine. Montparnasse, on the Left Bank, was at its best never more than a grassy mound, ironically nicknamed 'Mount Parnassus' after the Greek mountain sacred in legend to Apollo and the Muses, who presided over the arts and inspired mankind. For a few extraordinary years, through the 1920s and into the mid-thirties, Montparnasse lived up to its illustrious name, as the cafés became meeting places for artists, writers and composers, from eastern and central Europe and from the States, who had settled in Paris. It gathered momentum when on a December afternoon in 1923, the old Rotonde café, refurbished and enlarged, with an art gallery and a jazz band, gave a re-opening party. Not long after, other cafés in the Boulevard du Montparnasse, the Dôme and the Coupole, also became 'cafés of the arts'.

These years in the twenties were mad years in Paris, *les années folles*. Art was fashionable and it seemed that Montparnasse was where everything was happening, where you could meet painters such as Kandinsky, Klee or Matisse; where James Joyce, Hemingway, Cocteau, Scott Fitzgerald were among the writers drinking in the cafés, alongside composers such as Stravinsky and Manuel de Falla; where even the great Russian film director, Eisenstein, might drop in.

Little is left now of the brilliance that was Montparnasse, although the Coupole still attracts writers, film directors and pop stars, and you can hardly see through the windows of the Caméléon, a small local restaurant, so covered are they with posters advertising private art shows. There are still artists' shops in some of the side streets, such as the august Lucien Lefebure-Foinet, an emporium with formidable arrays of pallette knives, brushes, easels and everything a young or old master could possibly need.

To capture something more of the old Montparnasse of the twenties you have to go a mile or so to the south-west of the cafés, to find the narrow Passage Dantzig. Pushing open wrought-iron art nouveau gates covered in ivy, you enter a quiet rather overgrown garden of rose-bushes and trees, with cats peering round pieces of sculpture, half-hidden in the undergrowth. The garden belongs to a strange completely round building, *La Ruche*, the 'beehive', which at one time throbbed with the most advanced ideas in art. Léger, Chagall, Soutine, Zadkine all rented studios in *La Ruche*, to be followed before long by Picasso and Braque who moved here from Montmartre. The studios are still reserved mostly for working painters and sculptors, but the place seems to be remote now, haunted by the past, with a discernible aura remaining from the time when it was a hotbed of some of the most exciting ideas in art anywhere in the world.

Artists not only work in their studios, they live and love in them. Paris offers us the possibility of relating to the lives and personalities of some of the artists who lived there because it is so rich in personal one-artist museums, often housed in the same studios where the artist lived and worked. Many great artists have made their homes in Paris but if one had to be singled out, then Paris is above all the city of Pablo Picasso. He lived here for much of his life making some of his closest friends here, including Matisse, Braque, Apollinaire and the Hungarian photographer, Brassai. In Paris he painted what could be called his two most significant works, 'Les Demoiselles d'Avignon', in his small studio in Montmartre, and thirty years later one of the most powerful paintings of this century, 'Guernica', a personal cry of anguish, executed for the Spanish Pavilion of the 1937 Universal Exhibition in Paris, to show his horror at the bombing of the civilian population of Guernica, the Basque capital in Spain. A large stone tablet outside 7 Rue des Grands Augustins, a narrow road leading down to the Seine, notes that this was the studio where Picasso stayed for the longest period in his life, 1936–55, and where he painted 'Guernica'. So where else but in Paris could we expect to find Picasso's own private palace, one of the most beautiful museums ever dedicated to a single painter.

Picasso, who had many changes of address during his long life, now has permanently one of the best addresses of all, a lovely gracious mansion in the Marais, called the *Hôtel Salé*, because the first owner built it, in 1656, with the proceeds from a salt-tax concession granted by Louis XIV. As you walk up the staircase, wide and serenely proportioned, passing the delicate wrought-iron chandelier holding four long white candles, there is the warm feeling of being in someone's home. This seems to have been the intention from the start: Dominique Bozo, who was in charge of the ten-year project, called the museum, when it opened in 1985, *Picasso Chez Lui*, Picasso at home. And that is what it feels like.

So much has been done to make the Picasso Museum welcoming, almost as if you had been invited by Picasso himself. In the summer, the windows on the landing are wide open, unlike in most museums, letting in light and air, and Paris itself, the city where Picasso felt at home. Some of the things you see are particularly personal and poignant: there is a bronze cast of Picasso's right hand showing his short stubby fingers, the hand of a farmer or a craftsman. In an alcove on the back stairs is the chair he once used as an improvised pallette. Elsewhere there is a large photograph of him, by his friend Brassai, standing in the 'brilliant disorder', as Brassai described it, of his studio in the Rue des Grands Augustins. A glass case holds a swatch of his corrida tickets and some of his annual Communist Party membership cards, fully paid up, and made out of course to 'Comrade Picasso'.

As for the works of art in the museum, they are dazzling in the power and suppleness of the imagination they reveal. The earliest and perhaps the most affecting is a picture called 'La Fillette aux Pieds Nus', the little girl with bare feet, painted when Picasso was only fourteen, with astonishing sensitivity and depth of feeling for someone so young. The painting is now over ninety years old, with some of the oil paint flaked off, yet as revealing of life and compassion as when it was painted; and in keeping with the picture's simplicity and directness, no one has bothered to replace the cheap wooden frame, coming apart at the corners.

In other rooms in the museum, there are early works that are pivotal in the history of twentieth-century art: preliminary sketches show Picasso working on 'Les Demoiselles d'Avignon' (1906–7) and 'Homme à la Mandoline' (1911), a title altogether incidental because the picture is so fragmented as to be almost indeciferable, is close to pure abstract art. At other moments we are suddenly delighted by his humour and wit: a bicycle saddle with reversed handlebars over it flippantly evokes the 'head of a bull', his 'disjointed' portrait of Marie-Thérèse, one of the lovers in his life, is at the same time affectionate and funny. Then there is his own version, painted when he was nearly eighty, although you would never know it, of Manet's famous painting 'Le Déjeuner sur l'herbe', Picasso at his most Picasso.

Museums are merely a lot of lies, and the people who make art their business are mostly imposters . . . We have been fixed on a fiction instead of trying to feel what was the inner life of the men who painted.

Pablo Picasso

Paris honours another artist with a major one-man museum, Auguste Rodin, whom Sommerville Story calls 'the greatest sculptor since Michelangelo . . . the greatest thinker in stone of modern times . . .' He was born in Paris in 1840 and lived and worked there most of his life. In 1908 he rented what became his last home and studio, up to his death in 1917, in the Hôtel Biron at 77 Rue de Varenne by the corner of the Boulevard des Invalides. This is an imposing eighteenth-century mansion even by the standards of this district of Paris which is a repository of great Parisian residences. Artists and writers were allowed to use empty apartments in the house and while Rodin was there, Matisse, Rainer Maria Rilke, Jean Cocteau and Isadora Duncan at times shared it with him.

The rooms of the Rodin Museum leave a disarming impression of how Rodin worked, in the midst of a chaotic array of unfinished clay figures on turntables, sketches and work at different stages in stone, marble, plaster and terracotta. Finished pieces, 'Danaid', the naked figure of a woman with long flowing hair, emerging straight out of a rough unpolished block of marble, the 'The Crouching Woman', 'The Hand of God', seem vibrant with the extraordinary living energy that Rodin releases from inert stone and marble. His voluptuously erotic pieces, 'The Eternal Idol', a naked man reverently caressing a naked woman, and 'The Kiss', a copy of which is beyond the foyer of the Tate Gallery in London, are startling revelations of Rodin's obsession with the sensuousness of sex.

The small garden around the house, which has been restored in the eighteenth-century French style of landscaping, is an extension of the museum. At any turn you might see 'The Thinker', a 'Balzac', one of the 'Burghers of Calais' or some other marble or stone, mossy and weathered.

For the artist worthy of the name everything in nature has beauty, because his eyes, open to every truth on the outside, also reads the inner truth as in an open book. What is ugly is the false and the artificial, whatever aims at being pretty or even beautiful instead of being expressive.

Auguste Rodin

An art that somehow or other seems to belong to Paris is photography and it would be hard to find more elaborate and extensive photographic shops anywhere than *FNAC* in the Forum des Halles. Paris played a central role in the history of photography, taking what could be seen as the first experimental step in 1760 when Etienne de Silhouette took time off from his work as comptroller-general for Paris to adapt Aristotle's principle of the camera obscura. He reproduced people's profiles as an inexpensive kind of portrait, at the same time adding to his income and a word to the French and English languages. It was in Paris that the 'official birthday' of photography was celebrated on 19 August 1839, by Jacques Daguerre demonstrating to a joint meeting of the *Académies des Sciences et Beaux-Arts* his method of taking a daguerreotype.

Photography has flourished in Paris ever since. In 1898 Eugène Atget began one of the most remarkable photographic projects of all by taking the changing scenes in Paris, its streets, its buildings, its people, keeping a continuous photographic record for nearly thirty years. The memorial tablet to Atget, where he lived at 17 Rue Campagne-Première, proudly calls him 'the father of modern photography'. Long before *Life* appeared in the US, the Paris magazine *Vu* developed the 'picture-story', unfolding a whole narrative using photographs. Man-Ray, the New York artist who became a world-famous photographer in Paris, had his makeshift darkroom at 31 Rue Campagne-

Première in Montparnasse, just down the road from Atget's. Cartier-Bresson, the Hungarian photographer Brassaï, who worked with Picasso for a long period, and other outstanding photographers have added to the tradition of photography in Paris, which became one of the first cities to see this as a serious form of art.

During the month of November, every two years since 1980, Paris has become, in the words of Jacques Chirac himself, 'the international capital of photography'. The City of Paris puts up five million francs (about £500,000 or $825,000) for what it calls *Le Mois de la Photo*, a major biennial show during which for one month there are photographic exhibitions everywhere, in the big museums and in small private galleries, such as the prestigious gallery run by Agathe Gaillard on the corner opposite the Pont Louis-Philippe, a gallery with monotonal grey walls and grey furniture, as the best background for showing black-and-white photographs. 'Of all the arts which flourish better in France than in Britain', reported *The Independent* in 1987, 'Photography is the most striking.'

It was in Paris that an audience paid for the first time to go to a cinema. It happened on 28 June 1895 at the *Grand Café*, 14 Boulevard des Capucines, almost opposite where twenty years earlier the first impressionist exhibition was held. Louis and Auguste Lumière from Lyon gave a public showing of films. It was a spectacular success and a stone tablet marks the spot. So not surprisingly Parisians are 'movie mad': there is a bigger choice of films in Paris than anywhere else in the world. One cinema, the Cosmos, shows only films from the USSR. Three cinemas show only old American films. Another cinema specialises in series such as the old Chaplin or Buster Keaton films, or the Orson Welles films. And Paris has the most beautifully exotic cinema anywhere. The *Pagode* is in part of the original Chinese pavilion built for the 1900 Universal Exhibition, with the entire roof specially imported at the time from China. The whole of the auditorium is decorated with delicate oriental carvings, a Japanese tearoom leads off the foyer and on the opposite side there is a Japanese tea-garden.

The Cinémathèque Française, founded by Henri Langlois in 1936, was the first of its kind and its film library in the Palais de Chaillot is considered by film archivists to be the best there is.

Movies in Paris are treated as subjects for serious discussion, no less than art exhibitions and literature. The new Musée d'Orsay has a film department relating to film as an art form, that influences by its very nature the evolution of painting and sculpture.

Paris has a long tradition of spending lavishly on the arts but never before as much as in the 1980s. The city's planning department, working amid the caryatids, statues, coffered ceilings and florid chandeliers of the ostentatious Hôtel de Ville, the Paris town hall, gets frequent proposals for new museums. £500 million (about $800 million) is budgeted for just one project alone, François Mitterrand's scheme for the Louvre. Some doubts are being voiced whether all this can be afforded, and inevitably vote-catching political considerations come into the picture. So it is possible that even Paris may have to rein back for a while on expenditure on culture.

But the glass pyramid in the great palace courtyard of the Louvre will probably be completed and in spite of the controversy over it, there is also a lot of support and enthusiasm. On the other side of the Seine, the Musée d'Orsay is recognised everywhere as a marvellous triumph of vision and boldness. The Pompidou Centre continues to play to packed houses. Everyone finds the new Picasso Museum a place of wonder and delight, 'a textbook essay in sensitivity . . .' commented Waldemar Januszcza in *The Guardian*, '. . . one of the finest museums I have ever visited.' The wind is set fair to keep Paris in the lead, not only in Europe but throughout the world, as the first city for art and artists.

The Gare d'Orsay becomes the M'O

BOOKS
AND
WRITERS

In the middle of the Boulevard Raspail, where it is crossed by the Boulevard du Montparnasse, is a strange monument, more than 2m high (about 7ft) by the greatest of all French sculptors, showing one of the greatest of all French novelists clearly holding his erect penis under a heavy cloak. That is how the guide to the 1986 Rodin exhibition at the Hayward Gallery in London plainly describes Rodin's famous statue of Honoré de Balzac. Contemporary photographs show that Rodin worked on the statue by producing a naked study of Balzac in that stance and then 'draping' a long gown over it, leaving the outline of the figure clearly revealed.

Rodin himself had a compelling need for sex, describing it as a 'powerful awakener', demanding and distracting yet at the same time inspiring. In his memorial to Balzac he seems to relate the sexual gesture and the writer's compulsive pursuit of women, not always successful, to the driving creative energy that kept him writing all night, through well into the afternoon, keeping going with cup after cup of strong black coffee. It is not surprising that Rodin's statue was violently rejected by the French Society of Men of Letters who had commissioned it in the 1890s. The bronze cast, now looking up the Boulevard Raspail, was not erected until 1939.

I had to show a Balzac in his study, breathless, hair in disorder, eyes lost in a dream, a genius who in his little room reconstructs piece by piece all of society in order to bring it to tumultuous life before his contemporaries and generations to come.

Rodin, to Paul Gsell

Although Balzac was born in Tours in the Loire Valley, in 1799, and wrote some of his books, such as *Le père Goriot* and his *Tourangeau* novel *Le Lys dans la vallée*, not far away in the secluded Château de Saché, working as usual he said, 'night and day . . . taking refuge at the end of the château as if in a monastery', he really belongs to Paris. It was in Paris that he lived and worked for much of his life and where he died in 1850.

Along the Rue Bonaparte, a little way down from the animated Saint-Germain-des-Prés, is a narrow street, the Rue Visconti, not usually visited by tourists except for the very few who know how fascinating it is. Outside No 17 a tablet records that on the ground floor here Balzac set up the first of his financially ruinous projects, a printing press, while he lived in the flat above from 1826–8. Balzac was an unlikely businessman and when his printing press failed, leaving him once more heavily in debt, he again turned to writing to make some money. *Les Chouans*, the first novel under his own name, was published a year later in 1829 and was to become the first book in the greatest epic series of novels ever written, *La Comédie humaine*, the human comedy. Balzac planned 137 books of which ninety-one were written, in only twenty years, 1827–47.

A bad head for business and an irresistible love of women was tailor-made for financial disaster so Balzac, always on the run from debt-collectors at a time when you went to prison for debt, kept moving to different houses. One of his homes has been preserved by the City of Paris as a permanent Balzac museum. This would have appealed to Balzac's lively sense of irony because the Rue Raynouard, where it is situated, is named not after Balzac but after another writer, obscure and long-forgotten. Balzac lived from 1840–7 at No 47 Rue Raynouard in this well-off residential district of Passy on the west side of Paris. The feeling of tranquillity and middle-class security that you get as you descend the long flight of stone steps into a pleasant hidden garden and approach a comfortable country house is a long way from what it was for Balzac, when he lived here. He had moved in, once again to escape his creditors, even renting the house in the name of his housekeeper to avoid being traced.

47 Rue Raynouard is one of those intimate personal museums that Paris is so good at. On the wall in the hallway, is a photographic print of Balzac by Nadar from a daguerreotype taken in

1842, only a few years after the invention of photography. In one of the rooms is Balzac's foppish walking-stick, with its turquoise-studded gilt knob, and a clutch of the bills, summonses and distraints that followed Balzac everywhere he went. The small study, where he worked night and day on some of his finest novels, including his last two books *La cousine Bette* and *Le cousin Pons*, still seems occupied. His much-used large red and white coffee-pot is near at hand, and Balzac himself does not seem far away.

Around this little table lived all my miseries, all my tears were wiped away, my arms almost worn out by the effort of rubbing along it while I write.
Honoré de Balzac, in a letter to Madame Hanska

Leaving the house, you pass into the garden between two stone sphinxes. A small bust of Balzac peers out through the bushes. On the wall a panoramic bronze relief, at least six metres long (about 20ft), depicts some of the two thousand or so characters whom Balzac brings to life in the world he created in *La Comédie humaine*. Henry James, among others, considered Balzac the greatest of novelists; and sitting on a bench, where Balzac himself must have sat, in the shade of the trees of what seems like a country garden remote from Paris, you are near the source of what could fairly be called the beginning of the modern novel. In the house nearby, Balzac used his vision to give us a penetrating commentary on society, a literary approach followed later by generations of novelists writing in many different countries.

When Balzac left the Rue Raynouard in 1847 it was to move into a new house, which characteristically he never finished paying for, in a road, now the *Rue Balzac*, in a more fashionable district near the centre of Paris, between the Champs-Élysées and the Faubourg Saint-Honoré. For the remaining two or three years of his life he lived here in some style, his bookshelves decorated with tortoiseshell and bronze, his dining-room rich with carved oak panels and with plaster sculptures in his bathroom. Balzac had a taste for the grand manner.

At the same time in the 1890s when Rodin was working on his controversial sculpture of Balzac, he was commissioned to produce a monument to Victor Hugo. This was intended for the

Panthéon where Hugo is buried but when it turned out as a naked figure striding along, it was rejected. The plaster study for it is in the Rodin Museum described in chapter two and, like Rodin's monument to Balzac, a bronze casting is in the streets of Paris, set up in the Avenue Victor Hugo, which stretches all the way from the Étoile to the Bois de Boulogne.

Victor Hugo was born in 1802 only three years after Balzac, so they were contemporaries, although Hugo lived on until 1885, over thirty years after Balzac died, spanning the nineteenth-century as a towering figure in French literature and history. He is best known to English readers for his story of Quasimodo, the hunchbacked bell-ringer, and Esmeralda, the beautiful gypsy dancer in *The Hunchback of Notre-Dame*, a more evocative title than *Notre-Dame de Paris*, as it is called in the original. What is less well known is that Hugo's novel went a long way towards saving the great cathedral from the threat of demolition.

In the years after the Revolution, Notre-Dame had fallen into disrepair and in the early part of the nineteenth century it had even been sold to a demolition contractor. When Victor Hugo used it as the romantic setting for *Notre-Dame de Paris*, published in 1831, it focussed the attention of Parisians on what Hugo called 'this ancient queen of our cathedrals', and in time a decree was issued under the 'July Monarchy' of Louis-Philippe ordering the restoration of the whole edifice. Viollet-le-Duc, the French architect who knew so much about medieval architecture, laboured painstakingly for more than twenty years to repair and restore the cathedral. He did too much but Notre-Dame was saved for Paris and the world.

Victor Hugo is generally more known to us for his novels, particularly *Notre-Dame de Paris* and *Les Misérables* (which the National Theatre in London turned into a spectacularly successful musical), but his place in French literary history is more as the guiding spirit behind the nineteenth-century romantic movement in French *poetry*, as Wordsworth had been for the romantic movement in England. Hugo's range and power were much wider, as he was also a playwright and novelist, as well as a parliamentarian proclaiming the cause of liberty and justice. By the time of his death in 1885 he had become a national hero and was given a lavish ceremonial state funeral. Not long after, the City of Paris set up a permanent Victor Hugo Museum, more imposing than Balzac's modest house in Passy, situated in the south-west corner of the Place des Vosges, one of the grandest of the *grandes places* in Paris. The second floor of this rather gloomy mansion at No 6 Place des Vosges was Victor Hugo's home from 1832–48.

The Victor Hugo Museum embodies the extraordinary range of his genius. One room is given over to illustrations from *Notre-Dame de Paris*. Elsewhere are theatrical posters announcing his plays and records of his political life. Visitors are often surprised to find out that Hugo was also a considerable artist and the house displays many of his drawings and watercolours, strange 'dark night of the soul' landscapes and eerie castles. He also created strange abstract shapes by experimenting with ink blots.

Hugo was one of the most photographed of all writers. Early photographs show him as a good-looking romantic young man. As he gets older, photographs reveal him becoming powerful and impelling, leading to the marvellous charismatic bowed head we see in Rodin's arresting bronze. This is a far greater revelation of intellectual power than Rodin achieved in his famous sculpture 'The Thinker'.

We were at his house last Sunday week. A most extraordinary place, looking like an old curiosity shop, or the Property Room of some gloomy vast old Theatre. I was much struck by Hugo himself, who looks a Genius, as he certainly is, and is very interesting from head to foot. His wife is a handsome woman with flashing black eyes, who looks as if she might poison his breakfast any morning when the humour seized her.

Charles Dickens, from a letter to Lady Blessington, 27 January 1847

Voltaire (the name used by François-Marie Arouet) wry, detached, supremely intellectual with a dazzling wit, twice imprisoned in the Bastille because of his writings, is the archetypal Parisian. He was born in Paris in 1694 and died there as an old man, exhausted by too much of the social whirl, in 1778. His combination of worldliness and wit make Voltaire the most quotable of French writers and his aphorisms live on. Here are a few well-known ones: 'If God did not exist, it would be necessary to invent him'; *pour encourager les autres* ('In this country we find it best to shoot an admiral from time to time *to encourage the others'*); 'It is said that God is always on the side of the big battalions'; and the most famous defence of free speech, which is attributed to him, 'I disapprove of what you say, but I will defend to the death your right to say it.'

If we seek it out, we can see for ourselves in Paris, Voltaire's rapier quickness of mind and his cool cynicism, because they are extraordinarily alive in the statue of him, sitting down surveying life and society, by Jean-Antoine Houdon, the leading portrait sculptor in Europe at the time. Houdon had exceptional psychological insight which he could transpose into sculpture. He was even asked to visit America by the State of Virginia which commissioned from him a statue of George Washington. There are three places in Paris where we can see this statue of Voltaire. The original plaster is in the Mansart Gallery of the Bibliothèque Nationale, across the way from the Palais-Royal Gardens. The pedestal below is said to contain Voltaire's heart. A few minutes' walk away, in the upstairs foyer of the Comédie-Française, there is a bronze casting of the statue; and a rather chipped plaster cast of it looks on quizzically at art students in the entrance hall of the École des Beaux-Arts on the Left Bank.

The streets of Paris do well by Voltaire: the Boulevard Voltaire stretches nearly three kilometres (about two miles) from the Place de la République. There is a Rue Voltaire nearby and also an *impasse*, a cul-de-sac, named after him. But the most interesting is the *Quai Voltaire*, given its name in 1791, about twelve years after Voltaire's death, to commemorate one of the great Frenchmen of the century. Unlike the other places named after him, Voltaire actually lived here, for a short while in 1724 when he was thirty, at No 27, looking across the Seine to the Palais-Royal and the Louvre. The stone tablet on the wall records that he was back there some fifty-four years later, because this is where he died in 1778. Nowadays there is an attractive busy restaurant on the ground floor of the building called, with some justification, *Restaurant Voltaire*.

Paris has a peculiar reverence for the theatre. Backstage at the Comédie Française, instead of the narrow dusty corridors, stairways and dingy dressing-rooms of most theatres, it is almost as spacious as the front of house. The *Foyer des Artistes* is like an elegant club for the players, a splendid drawing-room decked out with grand furniture, long drapes and marble busts of former stars. Some of this dignity and pomp is also displayed in the monument to Molière, a few minutes' walk away from the Comédie-Française, where the Rue Molière joins the Rue de Richelieu, an appropriate place since it was Richelieu's own theatre in the Palais-Royal that in the 1660s first gave a permanent home to Molière's company. The solemn statue seems less appropriate. Perhaps it was unfortunate to ask Visconti, the architect who designed Napoleon's majestic tomb in Les Invalides, to design a memorial to a great comedian and comic writer. Molière sits there sedately, holding a pen, high up on a pedestal, a fountain occasionally playing below, flanked by two listless women bearing scrolls on which are inscribed a list of his works.

Molière was a complete man of the theatre. 'He was a comedian from head to foot', it is recorded by a contemporary, an inspired stage director and a playwright of genius, with a masterly sense of timing and comic revelation. He was born in Paris in 1622 and at twenty-one abandoned a safe career to lead a company of itinerant players, adopting *Molière* as a stage name about the same time. *Le Bourgeois Gentilhomme*, the most performed of his plays, is the story of Jourdain, a snobbish social climber, who is astounded to learn from his philosophy tutor that he has been 'speaking prose' all his life without knowing it.

Paris commemorates its greatest man of the theatre with the Avenue Molière in the west of the city, where the Lycée Molière is a school named after him, the Rue Molière where he lived near his theatre in the Palais-Royal, and there is also the tiny Passage Molière near the Pompidou Centre.

In every *quartier* Paris pays hommage to literature. The city names wide avenues, tree-lined boulevards, squares and streets, not only after the expected generals and statesmen, as other cities do, but after writers and poets as well. Pierre-Augustin Caron de Beaumarchais, 1732–99, has his Boulevard Beaumarchais, leading north from the Place de la Bastille, and stands assured and confident, as he did in life, in a statue erected nearby in the Rue Saint-Antoine. French encyclopaedists describe Beaumarchais as a writer, adventurer and libertine, a fair comment on his life-style. He was married three times, always to rich women, undertook secret missions for Louis XV and Louis

Beaumarchais' carved doorway

XVI, and set himself up in 1770 in a fine mansion, not so far from the boulevard named after him, at 47 Rue Vieille-du-Temple. You can still see the exotic medusa-like wooden carvings on the door, one of the most outstanding doorways in the Marais. From here he made a fortune dealing in arms for the American War of Independence. Alongside all that, he found time to write sketches and plays.

We remember Beaumarchais most for two plays, *The Barber of Seville* and *The Marriage of Figaro*, which became much more famous as the operas by Rossini and Mozart. Figaro, jack-of-all-trades, wily and involved in complicated love-affairs, could be the real-life character of Beaumarchais himself.

The urban replanning in Paris after 1850 gave plenty of opportunities to honour nineteenth-century writers in street names. A little way east of the Place de la Bastille, the Rue Charles Baudelaire echoes the name of a writer who is sometimes regarded as the first modern poet because of the way he used any theme in his poetry, even the most sordid experiences. Baudelaire had a short life, 1821–67, and published only one collection of verse. But what a collection! *Les Fleurs du mal*, a title difficult to convey but perhaps 'the fruits of evil' comes near to it, contains haunting transcendent love poems alongside other poems exploring so openly another side of love, the degradation and voluptuous pleasures of sex, that it provoked a court order suppressing them as obscene.

There is a reminder of Emma Bovary's hopes to realise her dreams, through lovers who fell so far short of them, in the Rue Gustave Flaubert, off the Avenue de Wagram, one of the wide avenues leading north from the Étoile. It was given its name a few years after the author of *Madame Bovary* died in 1880.

The Avenue Émile-Zola, in the south-west of Paris, leading to the Pont Mirabeau and the Seine, was named in 1907. Zola died in 1902. A fat pear-shaped man, he somehow reconciled a humourless opposition to pleasure with taking a girl of twenty as a mistress, when he was already forty-eight, and having two children by her. His Paris flat was in the Rue Ballu, not far from the Moulin-Rouge in Montmartre, and the descriptions in his sociological novels of orgiastic life there in the 1890s, evoking the stale smells in the cafés of absinthe, cheap cognac and strong coffee, are so palpable that his books were banned in Britain.

There is a Rue Guy-de-Maupassant, after the famous short-story writer, who was Flaubert's godson and was published by Zola, on the edge of the Bois de Boulogne. And in the fashionable Parc de Monceau the statue of a beautiful languid woman, clutching one of his books, stretches out below his bust. Marcel Proust, 1871–1922, and his *Remembrance of Things Past*, is in turn remembered in the name of an avenue in Passy and in the Allée Marcel-Proust alongside the Champs-Élysées. A road is named after the first science-fiction writer, Jules Verne, as well as the restaurant on the second floor of the Eiffel Tower. And just south of Montparnasse, even a lesser writer, such as Alphonse Daudet, part of the literary scene in Paris in the late nineteenth century, has his own road.

Flaubert's satisfaction came forth in a torrent of violent language, in front of which dear Madame Daudet seemed to withdraw in terror. Zola took an altogether natural delight in how money and success had transformed his life-style. Turgenev, who has the early stages of gout, had come in his slippers.
Journal des Goncourt, 7 January 1876

Paris, as a place to be free and enjoy life, has so often attracted writers from other countries. Turgenev was one of the first Russian writers to become known outside Russia, particularly for his play *A Month in the Country*. As a young man, he fell in love with Pauline Viardot, a celebrated Spanish operatic prima donna, who was living in Paris and had married a Frenchman. By some amiable arrangement Turgenev kept a flat for over thirty years on the third floor of the house at 50 Rue de Douai in Montmartre, where Pauline lived with her husband. Eventually in 1871 he moved in there permanently and stayed for the last twelve years of his life, having dinner most Wednesday evenings with Zola and Flaubert in Alphonse Daudet's modest flat in the Marais.

As you could expect from the author of *A Tale of Two Cities*, which unfolds in London and Paris, Charles Dickens was often in Paris, and one evening found himself having dinner in the same house in Montmartre where Turgenev had his flat. Dickens had been invited by the Viardots specially to meet George Sand, the woman novelist, who not only adopted a

Marché de Buci near Saint-Germain-des-Prés

man's name but also wore trousers, which in the mid-nineteenth century was scandalous. However, Dickens was not amused and found her 'a singularly ordinary woman in appearance and manner'. He has no personal connection with the tiny Square Charles Dickens, hidden away at the bottom of the steps beside the Métro Passy, although it is strangely not unlike a gas-lit square in Victorian London.

A long time before Thackeray wrote his most successful novel, *Vanity Fair*, he considered himself more as an artist, going to an art school in London, then continuing at an atelier in Montmartre, just at that time becoming fashionable as a place for painters. Thackeray lived there for three years, 1834–7, enjoying the easy-going life and scraping a living out of journalism. His *Paris Sketch Book*, which is a collection of articles and stories rather than drawings, was in fact Thackeray's first full-length work. Some ten years later he again recalls his life in Paris, when he makes Becky Sharp, the calculating heroine of *Vanity Fair*, the penniless orphaned daughter of an artist and a French dancer.

Paris played an important part in the life of Oscar Wilde, one of the first of the Irish writers to live and work there. He went there in 1884 for his honeymoon, living comfortably in a suite of rooms at a hotel at the better end of the Rue de Rivoli, near the Place de la Concorde. His one-act verse drama, *Salomé*, which he actually wrote in French, was banned in England and was first performed in Paris, by the legendary Sarah Bernhardt. And near the end of his life, worn out by two years in prison with hard labour, for homosexual offences, he returned to Paris, in 1897, as the only place where he could live. There he wrote about his prison experiences in *The Ballad of Reading Gaol*, and died two years later, near Saint-Germain-des-Prés in what was then a shabby hotel, where he is said to have made his famous quip about the decorations: 'I can't stand this wallpaper. One of us will have to go!' Perhaps he would be less likely to complain now, as *L'Hôtel*, as his old hotel at 13 Rue des Beaux-Arts is called these days, has moved up into the four-star luxury class.

Henry James, born in New York, was one of the first of a succession of literary 'Americans in Paris'. He was partly educated there and spoke very good French. At thirty-two, in 1875, he settled in Europe and although he lived most of the time in

Aux Deux Magots, 'Le café littéraire'

London, Paris was a second home to him. He worked there as a journalist from time to time, contributing to American magazines and was in touch with eminent writers such as Flaubert and Turgenev. And he loved the Louvre through which, he wrote, he inhaled 'little by little a general sense of glory', a good way of describing the effect of great art. The greatest writer for Henry James was a Frenchman, always Balzac, whom he called 'the master of us all'.

It would be difficult to think of Gertrude Stein, who came to Paris from Pennsylvania, without her lifelong friend Alice B. Toklas, who arrived from San Francisco. They lived together in Paris from the early 1900s at 27 Rue de Fleurus, which leads straight down to the Luxembourg Gardens. Her home, which was also an art gallery, became a famous literary salon before World War I, and on into the twenties. The visitors' book (if she kept one) would have read like a *Who's Who* of avant-garde artists and expatriot American writers, with names in it such as Picasso, Matisse, Juan Gris, Hemingway and Sherwood Anderson.

Gertrude Stein's well-known book, under the enigmatic title, *The Autobiography of Alice B. Toklas*, published in 1933, was in fact her own memoirs. Her familiar 'stream-of-consciousness' poetry, full of repetitions and disconnections seems eccentric and affected but at the same time can carry with it an underlying effectiveness. Paris was the perfect place in the world for Gertrude Stein to live out her life, with its warm Jewish intellectual quality, progressive, worldly and generous.

Ezra Pound, the American poet born in Idaho, was a visitor to Gertrude Stein's literary salon. He had come to Europe in 1908, taught in London, done research at the Bibliothèque Nationale in Paris, before moving, in 1920, to live in Paris for about five years. As well as writing his own poetry, and T. S. Eliot believed he contributed more than any other poet to new forms of poetry this century, Pound spent much of his time in Paris helping other writers. Ernest Hemingway described *Bel Esprit*, an association which Ezra Pound formed to get other writers in Paris to contribute to a fund aimed at getting Eliot away from the bank he worked for in London, so that he had more time for writing poetry. As a result, we could say Paris contributed to the mainstream of twentieth-century English literature.

Ernest Hemingway was the prototypal 'American in Paris'.

He settled there at the beginning of the 1920s, considering it 'the town best organised for a writer to write in', where food and wine were cheap, cafés accommodating and where there were other writers to talk to. Hemingway and his wife Mary lived in various apartments, and one of the first was on the third floor of 74 Rue du Cardinal-Lemoine in the Latin Quarter, at the other end of the Rue des Écoles from the Sorbonne. His two-room flat made do for a lavatory with a container with disinfectant in it but, as he was to concede many years later, this was 'not uncomfortable to anyone who was used to a Michigan outhouse'.

Not much money was coming in, in those days, and Hemingway often went hungry, which he found an even greater hardship in Paris, where everywhere he went there was the enticing smell of food, from the shops and from tables on the pavement where people were eating. So he chose his routes carefully, as he walked, to avoid passing as many places as possible where you could smell things to eat.

It was better, of course, after he made his name with *The Sun Also Rises*, published in 1926 and called *Fiesta* in England, and as royalties flowed in, Hemingway used to stay uptown at the Hôtel Ritz in the Place Vendôme. This was a fantasy for him after his years on short commons, a paradise where an expansive dinner followed the statutory dry martinis and was capped by a succession of brandies. By then it was time for bed, on which there were four pillows filled with real goose feathers, he tells us, 'two for me and two for my quite heavenly companion'.

Later he repaid the Hôtel Ritz for the delights it had given him by setting out, he declared, when he entered Paris in 1944 as a war correspondent with the American army, 'to liberate the cellar of the Ritz'. In turn, the Hôtel Ritz showed its gratitude, or perhaps it was just good for business, by one day opening a *Hemingway Bar*. Georges, well known there after the war as bar chief, used to call Hemingway, with his patriarchal grizzly beard, *Papa* and would talk to him about Scott Fitzgerald and other American writers who had lived in Paris.

Hemingway tells us in *A Moveable Feast*, his reminiscences of his life in Paris in the twenties, that he first met Scott Fitzgerald in 1925 at a bar in Montparnasse. This was the year that Fitzgerald's most acclaimed novel *The Great Gatsby* was published. His first novel *This Side of Paradise*, written five years before when he was only twenty-three, had been an instant success, so when the two American writers met in Paris, Scott Fitzgerald was rich and famous. He had married Zelda, an exciting and beautiful woman, and together they had become symbols of the high living, big spending, wild party-going life of the twenties, in both Europe and the States.

Fitzgerald was born in Minnesota in 1896, which made him three years older than Hemingway. Nevertheless Hemingway describes him as looking 'like a boy with a face between handsome and pretty'. Scott and Zelda had an apartment at 14 Rue de Tilsitt in one of the most expensive districts of Paris near the Étoile, but this did not stop them also staying at the Hôtel Ritz. Hemingway writes about drinking champagne with Scott Fitzgerald, not at the Ritz this time, but on the terrace of the Closerie des Lilas, at the time the leading literary café on the Boulevard du Montparnasse. For Hemingway it was '. . . one of the best cafés in Paris . . . warm inside in the winter'. In the summer there were tables outside, as there still are, under the shade of the plane trees, looking up at the statue of Marshall Ney flamboyantly brandishing his sword.

The old Closerie des Lilas is rather grander these days but still has a friendly atmosphere, in which writers and film directors talk together, and offers succour to novelists and scriptwriters under stress with a special range of drinks listed as *Pour les lendemains difficiles*, for those difficult 'mornings-after'.

Literary cafés in Paris, like the coffee-houses in London in the seventeenth and eighteenth-centuries, were, and still are in some ways, places where writers both meet and work. 'I could always go to a café and write,' Hemingway recalls, 'and could work all morning over a *café-crème* while the waiters cleaned and swept out the café.'

During World War II, the literary and intellectual centre of Paris was focussed on the Café de Flore in Saint-Germain-des-Prés, mostly because it suited Jean-Paul Sartre to work there. Brassaï took a photograph in 1950 showing Picasso at the Flore, with his usual stumpy cigar, in intense conversation, completely ignored by people at other tables because at the Café de Flore it would have been artless to stare at a celebrity. For the record, it is reported that it was at this same café that Albert Camus tried to pick up Simone de Beauvoir unsuccessfully.

A few doors along the Boulevard Saint-Germain from the Café de Flore, facing the oldest church in Paris, L'Église Saint-Germain-des-Prés, *Aux Deux Magots* cocks a snook at the Flore by now calling itself *Le Café Littéraire de Saint-Germain-des-Prés*. True enough, there are usually men and women at tables on the terraces, reading, writing notes, novels, poems or at least a postcard to send home. And the special *Aux Deux Magots* coffee remains particularly good and distinctive; old men say that it has not changed for fifty years.

The literary *bar* in Paris was unexpectedly at 5 Rue Daunou, a few steps from the Opéra. Harry's Bar is an institution. Noel Coward, Hemingway, Scott Fitzgerald, James Joyce, Thornton Wilder, Liam O'Flaherty, Jacques Prévert are just some of the distinguished literary elbows that have been lifted here. The bar counter and the mahogany panelling on the wall were shipped to Paris from New York to create the authentic ambiance, in time for the opening on Thanksgiving Day, 1911. The son and grandson of the original barman, Harry MacElhone, now preserve the traditions of Harry's Bar and the memories of a time when some Americans came to Paris with at least one address engraved on their hearts, *Sank Roo Doe Noo*, and every taxi-driver knew where to take them.

Paris is still a city for bibliophiles. There are bookshops in nearly every *quartier*, some of them open late and are extraordinarily welcoming. In the more fashionable districts are well-designed spacious bookshops owned by publishers themselves, such as Gallimard and Julliard. Then there are the many specialist bookshops, covering particular interests from mysticism to the cinema. The Librairie Ulysse, at 35 Rue Saint-Louis-en-l'Ile, sells only travel books, its glass doorway a notice-board for offers or requests for lifts to places so remote that most of us have to look them up in a gazetteer.

There are bookshops combined with cafés or *salons-de-thé* and bookshops where it is not easy to get served because the staff are too busy writing or editing. La Hune is the bookshop with the perfect location, just between the Flore and Aux Deux Magots, the two literary cafés of Saint-Germain-des-Prés. A narrow spiral stairway in the shop leads up to a booklined loft, which may explain the strange name of this bookshop, as *la hune* is a nautical term sometimes used for a crow's-nest. Nor does La

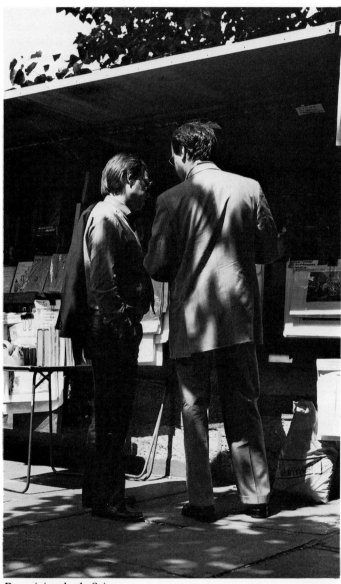

Bouquinistes by the Seine

Hune go in for much clock-watching, as it is open from Monday to Friday until midnight.

The most traditional booksellers of Paris, going back without a break to the seventeenth-century, are the *bouquinistes*, the bookstalls on the quays by the Seine, that, when closed, keep their stocks battened down into padlocked green boxes on the parapets. The *bouquinistes* regard themselves as the aristocrats of the book trade, just as Parisian taxi-drivers consider they have a divine right of the road. On a sunny afternoon, walking along the quays of the Left Bank where the *bouquinistes* set up their stalls, the Quai des Grands-Augustins, Quai de Conti, Quai Voltaire, can feel like browsing in paradise.

In the 1920s a few of the bookshops on the Left Bank were like literary clubs where writers met and read from the books they were working on. In 1919 a bookshop opened in the Rue Dupuytren, a tiny road hidden away not far from Saint-Germain-des-Prés. Its name, *Shakespeare and Company*, could seem affected, if its owner Sylvia Beach, the daughter of a Presbyterian minister from Princeton, had not befriended ex-patriot writers in Paris so generously and sympathetically. Hemingway said of her 'No one that I ever knew was nicer to me.' By 1921 Shakespeare and Company had moved nearby to less cramped premises in the Rue de l'Odéon where it remained well into the 1930s, offering to writers, once more in Hemingway's words, 'a warm, cheerful place with a big stove in winter, tables and shelves of books'. Sylvia Beach's real literary coup was to publish in 1922, for the first time in book form, James Joyce's *Ulysses*.

Sylvia Beach and most of the writers she befriended so warmly are long-since dead and although the cafés in Saint-Germain-des-Prés and the Boulevard du Montparnasse make the most of their place in literary history, the great days are over. Yet Paris continues to echo with the sound of writers, books and poems. In 1953, a *Shakespeare Garden* in the Bois de Boulogne was planted out with as many as possible of the trees, flowers and plants mentioned in Shakespeare's plays. *Place Colette* was named in 1966, at the corner of the Palais-Royal Gardens, as a tribute to Colette, whose flat during the last years of her life, at 9 Rue de Beaujolais, overlooked the gardens. In the mid-1980s, the *Square Jean-Cocteau* in the 15th *arrondissement* and the *Rue*

Shakespeare and Company

Jean-Cocteau in the 18th recall the gifted poet, novelist, play-wright and film director who died in 1963. And, under new management, *Shakespeare and Company* was reopened in 1964 by another American, George Whitman, said to be the great-grandson of Walt Whitman. Facing Notre-Dame, at 37 Rue de la Bûcherie, it is the most bookish of bookshops, where any writer or reader could feel at home, sitting on the bed in the Sylvia Beach Memorial Library upstairs, looking out through the small casement window, across the Seine at the towers of Notre-Dame.

We wish our guests to enter with the feeling they have inherited a booklined apartment on the Seine which is all the more delightful because they share it with others.
Shakespeare and Company

Alongside what may seem nostalgic reminders of the past, new shoots are appearing. Notably there is The Village Voice, well placed at 6 Rue Princesse, a short narrow street across the way from the old literary haunts of Saint-Germain-des-Prés. It is a bookshop combined with an art gallery, café and a centre for poetry readings, with every square foot of the small space made to work. The guiding light is a woman, a former translator for the United Nations, so she has a wide range of literary interests. Here there is no looking back but a positive commitment to new trends in writing: feminism, black writers and the Third World. The Village Voice has been described as *Génial*, not the same meaning as in English of course, but best translated here as – *Great!*

THE
SOUND OF
MUSIC

Saint-Saëns, who was organist at the Madeleine for twenty years, affirmed that music takes over where words leave off. To listen to 'Paris: the song of a great city', the musical tribute by Delius, is like going for a walk through the boulevards and along the Seine. Other composers, such as Maurice Ravel and George Gershwin, and also perhaps one singer more than others, Edith Piaf, have in their own ways sounded for us unmistakably the rhythm of Paris, its harmony and its discord.

Ravel spent his childhood mostly in Paris, where he entered the national *conservatoire* and studied composition under Fauré. Colette knew him: 'I listened to his music,' she said, 'out of curiosity to begin with . . . but soon became drawn to it because of its novelty.' He wrote 'La Valse' in 1920. Its sensuous harmonies, one moment flowing and lyrical, the next manic and frantic, then romantic and gracious, all the time underlined by a persistent dance rhythm, which never becomes monotonous as it does in his 'Boléro', reflect the hedonistic way Paris pours out energy just to give pleasure.

The same year that Ravel wrote 'Boléro', in 1928, George Gershwin came to Paris. He became a friend of Ravel's and studied composition for a short while with Nadia Boulanger, who was a kind of musical *guru* for many young American composers, starting with Aaron Copland. Gershwin had made a bid to be taken seriously as a composer with 'Rhapsody in Blue', performed four years before at Carnegie Hall in New York. The public loved it but most of the critics wrote if off as superficial, because at that time, it is said, serious composers in America had to be 'either European or dead, preferably both'. In Paris, like many other Americans, Gershwin gravitated to Harry's Bar near the Opéra. There was a piano in the basement and as usual

whenever Gershwin was near a piano, he played it, this time working out new themes.

Young Scott Fitzgerald chewed on his first Paris dry-martini olive here; Gershwin pounded the 'Downstairs Room' piano to pieces, putting together his 'American in Paris' . . .
Andy MacElhone, Harry's Bar

When Gershwin returned to New York he brought with him a collection of Paris taxi-horns. The new composition he had worked on was performed for the first time in December 1928 by the New York Symphony Orchestra, to which he had added *four Paris taxi-horns.* Gershwin had caught the true flavour of Paris in his few months there, the irresistible *joie de vivre* and incredulity of a young American let loose in the city, dodging the traffic, looking from side to side at the pretty girls, hailing taxis, all distilled into a tone-poem, 'An American in Paris'.

Edith Piaf was born in Paris in 1915. Her mother was an itinerant Italian street-singer, her father a circus acrobat from Normandy. She was on the streets when she was only fifteen and has told the story of how she came to Pigalle in Montmartre at that time, fell in love with Albert, a pimp, searching out for him rich women wearing jewellery, whom he enticed into a deserted cul-de-sac and robbed. Although she was discovered as a singer and was already known before the war, it was in the forties and fifties that she became a cult, not only in Paris but everywhere, as she sang in her poignant rasping voice 'La Vie en Rose', 'Milord', 'Je ne regrette rien' and other songs for which she sometimes wrote her own words. That voice, instantly recognisable, and her songs, embody the pleasures but more intensely the pain of Paris.

Near Père Lachaise, the cemetery where she is buried, there is now a Place Édith-Piaf and in the same district an Edith Piaf Museum has been arranged in two small rooms on the fourth floor of an old apartment block at 5 Rue Crespin du Gast, a shrine so it seems to a latter-day 'saint'. Once inside, which is possible only by appointment with the custodian, you can see some of her clothes, personal snapshots and even some of the letters she wrote to the *wives* of her lovers; Edith Piaf may have been minute, which is why she was called *La Môme*, the *Kid*, but

she had a generous heart.

George Gershwin is one of an astonishing list of composers from other countries who have come to Paris to make music, for Parisians were, in a sense, the internationalists of the musical world. They are not as musical as say the Italians or the Welsh, but they have offered the hospitable cosmopolitanism that musicians respond to. Debussy, who was a Parisian, is supposed to have said that 'music must modestly seek to please', and Paris has welcomed musicians as purveyors of pleasure.

Whenever I met Claude Debussy, it was somewhere within a cocoon of sound . . . his armchair always seemed to have a hazy aura of melody hovering over it.

Colette

Chopin of all foreign composers is identified with Paris. He was in fact half French and was born in Poland where he spent the first half of his life. For Parisians in the 1830s, when Chopin arrived in their city, he had all the qualities of the ideal romantic figure: he was twenty-one (what better age?), he was a 'poet of the piano', the perfect drawing-room instrument, he carried on a notorious love-affair with a controversial woman, the novelist George Sand, and he was consumptive. Inevitably he died young, aged thirty-nine, a piano being brought to his bedroom door so that he could hear on his death bed two of his 'Préludes', numbers *four* and *six* it was faithfully noted at the time. A plaque outside No 12 Place Vendôme, on the opposite side to the Hôtel Ritz, records that this is where it all took place, a fashionable address that would have pleased Chopin, who liked the company of aristocrats.

Chopin's funeral service was spectacular. It was held in the Church of the Madeleine, packed with an audience of four thousand listening to Mozart's 'Requiem', performed by the entire choir and orchestra of the Paris *Conservatoire*. After that, the Place Chopin in Passy, between the Seine and the Bois de Boulogne, is a rather modest square, although the Chopin monument in the Parc de Monceau more than makes up for that. Long ago forgotten, unknown these days even to most Parisians, it is worth a pilgrimage to see it: Chopin is seated at the piano, his left foot on the pedal, left hand poised over the

A Chopin Prélude in Parc Monceau

keys ready to deliver a passionate chord, as he looks soulfully down at the enraptured woman lying at his feet. Overhead a pretty winged angel in a seductively flimsy dress drops roses on the whole scene. More genuinely moving is the plaster cast of Chopin's left hand, surprisingly small but with very agile fingers, which is in the Renan-Scheffer Museum, south of Montmartre. A portrait of George Sand, his lover, is nearby.

His creation was immediate and miraculous; it came to him without his searching for it, without his foreseeing it. It was there on his piano suddenly, complete, sublime, or it echoed in his head during a walk, and then he was impatient to play it to himself.
George Sand on Chopin

Mozart as a pampered child prodigy of seven spent the winter of 1763 in Paris, staying at the home in the Marais of the Bavarian ambassador, the Hôtel de Beauvais, 68 Rue François-Miron. In the splendid *grande salle* on the second floor, Mozart gave his first public harpsichord recital in Paris, a great success, as his performances had been throughout the courts of Europe. The seventeenth-century mansion is rather run-down at the present time although, standing in the entrance looking through the beautiful peristyle of eight Doric columns, up to the salon where Mozart played, it is still possible to recapture its former elegance. The musical associations of the house continue during the annual Festival of the Marais in July each year, when recitals are given in the vaulted crypt.

Gluck, who was born in Bavaria, lived in Paris for nearly seven years, 1773–9, during the latter part of his life. Here where there was a tradition of operas in French rather than in Italian, Gluck left behind the Italian style with lots of songs that showed off the singers' voices, to write arias that brought out the drama and feeling of the libretto. Most of his earlier operas are forgotten now and Gluck's fame rests on the operas he wrote in Paris, particularly his 'Orpheus', rewritten in Paris in 1774, which is one of the earliest full-length operas still in the modern repertoire.

Musicologists consider that Gluck was the forerunner of Richard Wagner in the next century. Wagner also lived in Paris, during 1839, supporting himself by the drudgery of music-

copying and by arranging popular opera melodies of the day for the cornet, menial work for the composer who was later to write 'The Ring of Nibelung'. But that was already foreshadowed during those early days, because while he was in Paris Wagner wrote 'The Flying Dutchman', the first of his operas based on legend. Nearly thirty years later, in 1867, Wagner was back in Paris, living more comfortably, looking out over the Seine from the tall windows of the Hôtel du Quai Voltaire, while he finished writing one of his happiest works, 'The Mastersingers of Nuremberg'.

Two other famous composers of operas came to Paris in the nineteenth century but for entirely different reasons. One, an Italian, came to live there comfortably without working. By the time he was thirty-seven Rossini had already written thirty-six operas, including 'The Barber of Seville' to a libretto based on Beaumarchais' comedy. His last opera was 'William Tell' and after that he more or less stopped writing music, spending the last fifteen years of his life, 1853–68, in Paris enjoying food and wine.

In gratitude perhaps for the good life he had lived there, Rossini left all his money to the City of Paris to found a home for old musicians. Some time before then Paris had recognised the distinguished composer in their midst by naming a street the *Rue Rossini*, appropriately situated at the end of the Boulevard des Italiens, within easy walking distance of the Opéra. Gourmets are more at home with another tribute to Rossini's taste for good living. *Tournedos Rossini* belongs to the classic French *haute cuisine*: small round filet steaks garnished with truffles and sliced *foie gras*.

While Rossini was living an easy life in Paris, a German composer was also there, working hard, writing over a hundred operettas. Jacob Offenbach or, as the French call him, Jacques, was the son of a Jewish cantor in Cologne. He settled in Paris as a young boy and eventually became naturalised, earning a living as a cellist to begin with, before becoming, in 1847 when he was still under thirty, the conductor for the Comédie-Française. Perhaps this appointment gave him the insight into theatrical comedy that helped him to develop the style of the Parisian operetta, which has spoken dialogue as well as songs. It is possible to see his light operas, such as 'La Vie Parisienne' and

'Orpheus in the Underworld' as forerunners of the spectacular musicals staged on Broadway in the next century. A plaque on the column beside the door of 8 Boulevard des Capucines informs passers-by that Offenbach wrote his most ambitious opera here, 'Tales of Hoffman', inspired perhaps by looking at the Opéra just over the way, and finished it not long before he died in 1880.

For a long time opera meant more to the French than other kinds of music and it was even felt that a composer was hardly a composer at all unless he wrote music for opera. This goes back to the seventeenth century when another Italian, Jean-Baptiste Lully, was appointed the principal composer to Louis XIV. Lully collaborated with Voltaire, writing music for some of his plays, and then went on to write *tragédies en musique*, where the music took precedence over the libretto, which paved the way for the development of opera in France.

To see just how much opera meant in Paris by the late nineteenth century, look up the wide Avenue de l'Opéra and take in that grandiose Kubla Khan of a palace, the Paris Opera House. In comparison, the Royal Opera House in London, with its restrained classical façade, tucked away opposite a police station in Bow Street, is quietly self-effacing. Napoleon III and Baron Haussmann, his chief commissioner for Paris, had imperial ambitions for the city. Paris had become the centre of European music. So when they planned a new opera house, nothing could be too grand or too magnificent. 171 designs, including one by the Empress herself, were submitted in an open competition. Charles Garnier, a little-known architect aged only thirty-five, was unanimously selected by the jury.

The foundation stone was laid in 1862 and the Opéra was opened in 1875. Few architects have ever had so much expected of them so it is understandable that Garnier introduced an unrestrained mixture of styles, from Italy, Greece, the Near East, from anywhere where there was a tradition of palatial splendour.

The Opéra was intended for state occasions, when making an entrance was more important than seeing the show. Nor is it easy for any show to follow on after the Grand Foyer, 54m long (about 175ft), 18m high (nearly 60ft), with polychrome marble columns three storeys high, great sweeping balustrades of Algerian onyx and mosaics and statuary everywhere. At times

the effect is diminished by bedraggled crowds of tourists in jeans or shorts, clicking away with their cameras. Then the whole thing can seem like wildly over-gilded kitsch. But the Grand Foyer is to be imagined on a regal occasion, bedecked with pomp and ceremony, the fabulous stairway flanked on both sides by a resplendent guard of honour.

If the world were ever reduced to the dominion of a single gorgeous potentate, the foyer of the Opéra would do very well for his throne room.

Henry James, *Parisian Sketches*

At first sight the auditorium seems smaller than might be expected. It does in fact seat only 2,200, because so much space in the building has been sacrificed to the Grand Foyer and the stage itself, which is big enough to mount a spectacle with a cast of nearly five hundred. In 1964 Chagall painted a circular tableau for the ceiling of the auditorium, which is deplored by some critics. Yet Chagall's fairy-tale fantasy suspended over all the gold and red plush can have a welcome lightness and delicacy. Nor does it seem so out of place. For although the whole place belongs to an era that has passed, and the red carpet in the auditorium has threadbare patches, an evening at the Opéra can still seem like an evening in fairyland.

In the years just before World War I attention began to move away from the Opéra to the new Théâtre des Champs-Élysées, as Paris was overwhelmed by the performances of the *Ballets Russes* created by the Russian impresario Serge Diaghilev in 1911. Everything was new. Diaghilev collected around him an incredible array of talent and over the next few years audiences marvelled at the dancing of Pavlova and Nijinsky among others, to new music commissioned by Diaghilev from composers such as Ravel and Manuel de Falla, but especially Stravinsky, in sets designed by Picasso, Braque, Rouault and other experimental painters.

After he met Diaghilev, Igor Stravinsky made Paris the centre for his new style of music which lay aside conventional harmony, rhythm and form. This was to become a dominant influence in twentieth-century music, although to begin with audiences were outraged. The first performance in 1913 of

Fête de la Musique

Stravinsky's 'The Rite of Spring' was hooted off the stage at the Théâtre des Champs-Élysées. After it was all over, we are told that Stravinsky, Diaghilev, Nijinsky and Jean Cocteau, who had designed the sets, took a subdued silent taxi ride round the Bois de Boulogne to calm their nerves. It is not by chance that Stravinsky and Picasso were friends: they both had to endure waiting for the public to catch up with their advanced ideas.

The charming Place Igor-Stravinsky with a fountain and a pond full of psychedelic fantasies is next to the Pompidou Centre; and what better place than alongside a square named after Igor Stravinsky could they have put the IRCAM studios, run by Pierre Boulez as the most advanced centre for experimental music?

Musical life in Paris has for centuries been enriched by the

organs in its churches and by composers who have come to the city to play on them. The marvellous organ in Notre-Dame was completely restored in 1863 by a master, Aristide Cavaillé-Col, a member of a family that had been building organs since the early eighteenth century. Musicians were eager to play on the new organ, and among the first were César Franck, Camille Saint-Saëns, Anton Bruckner and Marcel Dupré, for some years acting-organist in the great cathedral.

César Franck, who was born in Belgium, played another fine Cavaillé-Col organ, in the organ loft of Sainte-Clotilde, a rather sombre church in the Rue Las-Cases in the fashionable 7th *arrondissement*. Franck was organist here for nearly forty years, living a simple frugal life, like a saint, getting up before dawn and spending much of his time in meditation. His music has a mystical ecstasy which made Debussy call him 'one of the greatest'.

Saint-Saëns was appointed organist at the Madeleine, the vast Greek temple of a church looking up the Rue Royale towards the Place de la Concorde, in 1857 when he was only twenty-two. He had been a child prodigy who had given his first public piano recital at the age of ten.

It will perhaps be accepted that I have some knowledge and understanding of the mysterious depths of an art in the midst of which I have lived since I was a child like a fish in water . . . Music begins where speech leaves off; it voices the ineffable, reveals feelings within us we had not suspected, communicates sensations and states of being that no words can express.
Camille Saint-Saëns, *Portraits et Souvenirs*

Saint-Saëns remained organist at the Madeleine for about twenty years, writing music almost every day of his life, until he died in 1921, aged eighty-six. We remember him most perhaps for his symphonic poem 'Danse macabre', which manages to sound like the jangling of skeletons in a churchyard, and for his opera 'Samson and Delilah'. Others may nod gratefully in his direction when they see on the menu of a grand restaurant, *suprême de volaille Saint-Saëns*: truffle and *foie-gras* fritters, cock's kidneys and asparagus tips served as a garnish for chicken breasts.

Some years after Saint-Saëns, his pupil, Gabriel Fauré, who in turn taught composition to Ravel, as noted earlier, became organist at the Madeleine. Fauré is one of the most refined composers this century, with long elegantly sustained melodies, rather English in feeling, anticipating Vaughan Williams, Benjamin Britten and Lennox Berkeley.

The church of Saint-Sulpice, not far from Saint-Germain-des-Prés, was rebuilt between the seventeenth and eighteenth centuries and is sometimes called the cathedral of the Left Bank, because of the vastness of its classical architecture. The church can seem heavy and plodding and dull: the art critic John Russell described its twin towers as looking like 'municipal inkwells'. But the organ loft is superb, with beautiful wood carvings. The organ, bigger even than the organ of Notre-Dame has 6,588 pipes and is outstanding in tone and quality. The great organist and teacher Charles Widor was organist here and was succeeded by his most distinguished pupil, Marcel Dupré.

Facing the Hôtel de Ville, the town hall of Paris, the classical façade of Saint-Gervais-Saint-Protais rises up in three tiers. The organ, built in 1601, is the oldest in Paris and is connected with one of the longest dynasties in the history of music, extending over two hundred years. Nine members of the Couperin family were one after the other organists at this same church, from about 1650 to 1850. François Couperin, who became organist in 1696, is the best known because of his harpsichord music. Just behind the church a stone tablet on the wall of a building records that this was the home of *Les Couperins – Musiciens Français*, and a little further away is a cool leafy square called *Square Couperin*.

There are more beautiful places in Paris where you can hear music than in most cities, because so many churches double as concert halls. The pretty garden in the Square Viviani has on one side one of the best views of Notre-Dame, across the Seine. On the other side is a view which the conservative Michelin guide awards the accolade of three stars: through a curtain of trees, one of which is said to be the oldest tree in Paris, planted at the beginning of the seventeenth century, the clear white of Saint-Julien-le-Pauvre stands out like some ancient shrine. It was built between 1165 and 1220, when Notre-Dame itself was being built, and is the oldest church in Paris that has remained intact, almost unaltered. This small intimate church could have

been built for chamber music, for which it is now used every summer, with recitals by string quartets and by guitar and lute duos.

There is a long tradition of concerts in Saint-Eustache, the great cathedral-like church of Les Halles, which was the old Paris food market. Berlioz conducted here in 1855 the first performance of his 'Te Deum', with 950 performers. A bust of Liszt in the church commemorates his conducting rehearsals there. Near it is a bust of Rameau who is buried in the church and gave his last organ recital here, high up in the great organ loft.

Saint-Louis-en-Ile, the only church on the Ile St-Louis, is used more as a concert hall than a church. Any afternoon you would find rehearsals in progress for a concert or an oratorio to be given that evening. Saint-Séverin, for centuries the parish church of the Left Bank, offers some of the best choral music in Paris, with the additional delight of being able to walk through the sequence of delicate columns that make up the ambulatory behind the altar.

The most luminous place imaginable where you can attend a concert is the Sainte-Chapelle, preserved in a remote courtyard beside the Palais de Justice on the Ile de la Cité. It was built in the mid-thirteenth century to house the 'crown of thorns', the 'true cross' and other holy relics that Louis IX, Saint Louis, had purchased from the Emperor of Constantinople.

The Sainte-Chapelle is a joyful celebration of the discovery of flying buttresses, which enabled the interior supporting structures to be thinned right down, so that the mass of stone wall gives way to the radiance of walls made up almost entirely of stained glass windows. From near the ground these rise up 12m (almost 40ft) with the slenderest of mullions in between. There are over six hundred square metres (more than seven hundred square yards) of stained glass and much of it goes back to the thirteenth century. The effect is arresting in its daring and radiance, like walking into a medieval illuminated manuscript.

The Sainte-Chapelle is small enough to be a music room and the acoustics are extraordinary. A solo voice or a single instrument sounds as if it is all around you. Concerts here are mostly of medieval music or French baroque music of the seventeenth century, sometimes with English Elizabethan music by William

Byrd, John Dowland or Thomas Morley. But even hearing Thomas Morley's 'It was a lover and his lass' sung in a French accent takes away nothing from the unforgettable experience of listening to early music performed in this marvellous setting.

In the centre of Paris is a collection of old musical instruments, some of them similar to ones used for concerts in the Sainte-Chapelle. You can wander about on your own, no security guards watching your every move, and look at the simple perfection of a row of five violins made by Antonio Stradivari, from Cremona in north Italy, 1644–1737, at Marie-Antoinette's harp, Paganini's guitar, the portable clavichord believed to have belonged to Beethoven, an original alto-saxophone made in Paris in 1867, by its inventor Adolphe Sax, and over four thousand other musical instruments dating from the sixteenth century up to the present. This *Musée Instrumental* has to be searched for by going through the rather institutional national music *conservatoire* at 14 Rue de Madrid, off the fashionable Boulevard Malesherbes.

A very diferent musical museum is hidden away at the end of a narrow cul-de-sac, the Impasse Berthaud, on the opposite side of the Rue Beaubourg to the Pompidou Centre. The Mechanical Music Museum, privately owned by a devoted collector, was opened in 1983 by Jacques Chirac. Here is a mechanical accordion player, a mechanical violin and even a complete Kentucky jazz group, life-size, tapping their feet and beating out the rhythm on a drum, all operated by putting in a coin.

Coin-operated mechanical jazz groups aside, Paris has had the right to call itself the second home, after the States, of live jazz, ever since it was introduced here, it is claimed, by Josephine Baker, the girl from St Louis, Missouri, in the musical 'Nègre' where she danced naked. There are some fifty places in Paris where jazz is performed, some still in the old cellars off the boulevards Saint-Germain and Saint-Michel, where acoustics and atmosphere lend themselves so well. Le Caveau de la Huchette, in the Rue de la Huchette, has been serving up straight mainstream jazz since the early existentialist days of Jean-Paul Sartre. In those days in Paris, listening to jazz seemed the easy non-intellectual approach to existentialism for anyone who wanted to be in touch but could not handle the abstruse philosophical concepts.

Nowadays big names, such as Dizzy Gillespie, are as much at home playing in Paris as they are in the USA. Irvin Stokes, the black trumpet player from Brooklyn, summed it up: 'Jazz belongs in both places. In the States you get up in the morning and you start playing: here in Paris maybe you get dressed first.'

More advanced than the most progressive jazz is the experimental music going on at IRCAM, the *I*nstitut de *R*echerche et *C*oordination *A*coustique/*M*usique. Pierre Boulez, France's leading contemporary composer, has assembled, in an underground annex to the Pompidou Centre, an acoustical laboratory with banks of synthesisers and computers. Here, as Boulez puts it, 'artists use forms of musical expression right to the limits of possibility'. Much more than electronic music, it is an attempt to probe into the future, to listen to the sounds of music to come in the next century.

A unique music festival takes place in Paris every summer on the 21 June. This day has been declared by the city *La Fête de la Musique*. For the whole day all concerts in Paris, in the churches and concert halls, are free, as the cost is borne by the State. It starts the previous evening with music in the streets, under the arcades in the Place des Vosges, in the squares, or wherever musicians gather together to perform classical, jazz or choral music.

A new Paris opera house will be opening before very long in the Place de la Bastille, where the best seats will cost about a third of what they cost at the Opéra. This is intended to make opera as available and popular as the Pompidou Centre has done for modern art. Also being built is *La Cité de la Musique*, a musical 'city', at Villette on the edge of Paris to the north. When this is ready the national *conservatoire* will be moved there, with much better facilities, and also the museum of musical instruments which will be enlarged so that there is more space to see and enjoy its outstanding collection.

The sound of music never seems far away in Paris´ and not only during *La Fête de la Musique*, when Paris becomes an open musical city. At other times as well there is no limit to the different kinds of music available, from medieval motets at the Sainte-Chapelle to mainstream jazz in cellars on the Left Bank to composers conducting in front of banks of computers in one of the futuristic studios of IRCAM.

THE ART OF EATING

With all the immigrants in New York there is no shortage of foreign restaurants, including French ones of course. In London menus in French remain an acknowledgement of the classic language of gastronomy. Yet as you compare the different experiences, a wide gulf still separates eating in Paris from eating in other cities.

Elizabeth David has described a curious experience that many people have had in restaurants: French dishes cooked, for example, by a Pole or an Italian in Paris, seem to taste more French than the same dishes cooked by a genuine French cook in say London or New York. *Rosbif* in Paris never tastes the same as roast beef in London; an omelette in an ordinary Paris bistro can, if all goes well, seem more like a feast than an omelette in a much grander restaurant in New York.

Why is there this difference that so many of us have noticed? Elizabeth David puts it down partly to 'the climate, the soil, the ingredients, the saucepans, the stove, even the way of arranging the food upon the serving dish, of folding the napkins and setting the table . . .' The geographical position of France gives that country a greater daily variety of fresh fruit, vegetables and other produce, than most other countries. Such things we can see for ourselves but there is something else, less easily definable: it is the French attitude towards eating. You pick it up sometimes in the very smell of their kitchens, while cooking is going on, or in the slight flourish with which a plate of food is placed in front of you. When Parisians scan a menu in a restaurant it is not a casual relaxed affair. Conversation stops and there is a purposeful, even intense concentration.

. . . the French give a higher priority to food than to sex, fame, health or money . . .

Elkan Allan in *The Independent*

'A la carte' in the Place de Passy

Great French cooks, even ordinary housewives sometimes, will talk about eating as a creed. The conversation round a dinner table will often have the same tonality and instead of saying something is 'delicious' or 'very good', there could be an attempt to look for the underlying truth beyond. When Charles Barrier, one of the great chefs of France, talked to me about food, it sounded like Zen in the art of cookery. For Barrier it is an esoteric knowledge that enables him to summon up clean, pure flavours that both harmonise and remain separate, keeping you in a state of constant enchantment. Colette believed that the mere *cleaning* of truffles is such an art that she would not delegate it to anyone else. She would herself put half a bottle of dry champagne into an iron stew-pan, adding some lightly browned bacon fat before bringing the mixture to the boil and tossing in the truffles.

Even a king of France, Henri IV 1589–1610, has a place in French cookbooks. *Poulet Henri IV*, a classic recipe, is a reminder of the King's pious wish that 'No peasant in my Kingdom should be so poor that he cannot have a chicken in his pot every Sunday.' The royal recipe calls for a chicken stuffed with liver and ham and cooked in wine.

More than other countries, France has a strong tradition of regional dishes. In some cases this is based on locally available food, such as *bouillabaisse*, the Marseillais fish stew made from the great variety of fish sold by local fishermen. In other cases the character of the people living in the region dictate a dish. A traditional dish in Alsace, a region with historic links with Germany, is *choucroute garnie*, the formidable Teutonic dish of pickled white cabbage, usually with spiced pork sausages.

In Paris it is possible to do a complete gastronomic tour of the regions of France. La Chope d'Alsace, in the Carrefour de l'Odéon by the Boulevard Saint-Germain, serves hundreds of customers, every day of the week up to two o'clock in the morning, six different kinds of *choucroute garnie*. A dozen or more restaurants serve *cassoulet*, the traditional stew from Languedoc, made with white haricot beans, pork sausages and other meats. The Ducs de Bourgogne in the Place d'Anvers in the 9th *arrondissement*, a warm family restaurant with old beams and hunting trophies, is one of several restaurants in Paris offering Burgundian dishes, which as you would expect with food from Burgundy are cooked in wine. Chefs from all the fourteen geographical regions of France either own or cook in the kitchens of restaurants in Paris and for weeks on end you could every day try a different regional speciality.

The French attitude towards eating can take in even the most ordinary food. As far back as 1821 a cookery writer calculated that there were '685 ways of dressing eggs in the French kitchen', starting with *oeuf à la coque*, the basic boiled egg. Nothing complicated about that you would think, but even here Elizabeth David quotes from Madame Saint-Ange's *Livre de Cuisine*, giving *five* carefully described methods of boiling an egg. At the Jamin in Paris, in the Rue de Longchamp, one of the top-rated restaurants in the whole of France, the humble mashed potato becomes a delicate rich purée as it is blended with the best Normandy butter. Elsewhere unpromising cabbage is given special treatment by Alain Senderens, *chef de cuisine* at the Lucas-Carton, a restaurant of the highest quality near the Madeleine. Here, amidst original turn-of-the-century decorations, cabbage is served lightly steamed and transformed into a memorable experience as *foie gras de canard aux choux à la vapeur*.

As for *tripe*, a food that in England is so plebeian that the word has become slang for a 'load of rubbish', it has been elevated in France to a gastronomic adventure for the brave or robust. *Tripes à la mode de Caen* is tripe cooked slowly, for twelve hours at least, with ox feet, onions, leeks, cider, Calvados and other ingredients, according to the inspiration of the chef. This speciality from Normandy has been served since the reign of Louis-Philippe, in the early part of the nineteenth century, at the Pharamond, a distinguished restaurant in the Rue de la Grande-Truanderie near Les Halles, the former Paris food market.

It was a piece of cheap cut of beef, presumably cheek, richly stewed and then strewed with poached marrow, quite the most satisfying dish I have had in a long while, the detail of the garnish lifting it out of the home-cooking class.

Fay Maschler in *The London Evening Standard*,
(on eating in Paris at the Grand Véfour)

Paris gathers in cheese from all the regions of France, for cheese here is not an afterthought or an option after a dessert, but usually an obligatory course served after the main course. The average Parisian eats between two and three times as much cheese as a Londoner and takes it much more seriously. Winston Churchill was quoted as saying, during the last war, 'A nation that makes more than 180 different cheeses cannot die!' In fact the current A-Z of French cheeses runs to nearly four hundred different kinds. Like the wines of France, cheeses vary according to the climate, the soil and the lie of the land.

There are a few restaurants in Paris, such as the *Fromagerie* near the famous food market in the Rue Mouffetard, where every dish is a cheese dish: cheese soup, a cheese tart, roquefort paté, cheese soufflés and many more, enough to fill a double-page menu. Every district in Paris has a specialised *fromagerie* selling nothing but cheeses and butter, some of them owned by a *maître fromager*, who will discuss and recommend a cheese with the same considered solemnity as a master of wine will talk about varieties of grapes and vintages.

The most eminent cheese shop in Paris, at 41 Rue d'Amsterdam near the Gare Saint-Lazare, is Androuet which has been there since the beginning of the century. They sell and export all over the world some 150 different cheeses. In the restaurant above a generous sampling of all the cheeses in the shop costs about £20 ($33). Pierre, the *maître fromager*, will bring on a seemingly endless series of straw-lined wicker platters of cheeses which he will present and explain in detail before serving. The sequence begins with mild cream cheeses, followed by cheeses made from ewes' milk, then maybe a platter of thirty or so varieties of goat cheese, then a bewildering selection of blue cheeses, and always ends with a platter of specially strong cheeses, the only kind with which butter is respectfully recommended.

The famous *baguettes* of Paris are not what they used to be. Parisians who can be so critical about every detail of what they eat can be extraordinarily indifferent to the quality of bread. Even quite good restaurants will serve steam-baked tasteless pappy *baguettes*. That is the rule; but dotted around Paris are occasional old-style bakers where bread is still baked in wood-fired ovens and comes out crunchy and full of flavour. They announce this proudly by a notice on the door: *Pain cuit au feu de*

Buying a baguette

bois. Or you can recognise them by the queues outside.

With all the many *boulangers* in Paris, one stands out as the most famous of all. The Poilâne bakery at 8 Rue du Cherche-Midi, near where it crosses the Boulevard Raspail, is a family business that has been going since the mid-1930s. Outside this tiny shop there are always long queues, as if there were a famine in the land. The small cellar below is the bakery, where one baker a time, working in shifts, kneads dough by hand, sliding the loaves on long trays into a wood-fired oven. This goes on twenty-four hours a day, every day except Sunday, so that fresh Poilâne bread is always available, because nowadays they supply shops and restaurants throughout Paris. Poilâne bread has become a cult and a refreshing indication that an ever-increasing number of Parisians expect to get pleasure even from the bread they eat.

Quentin Crewe, who wrote *Great Chefs of France*, believes that 'France is the only western country where cooking, and indeed eating, is an art'. Hence it is not by chance that for the French, for longer than living memory, the name *Michelin* has been more renowned for its star system of rating restaurants than for tyres. What started out as a convenient guide for motorists, long ago became the most respected arbiter of the art of cooking in French restaurants. Full-time inspectors, always completely anonymous, apply uncompromisingly strict criteria. Michelin's highest order of merit is three stars and while there is no official limit to how many highest awards can be given, only eighteen restaurants in the whole of France received this supreme accolade in 1987, less than the number of Orders of Merit bestowed by Queen Elizabeth II on her most distinguished subjects.

Out of the twelve thousand eating places in Paris, at the last count, only *four* reach up to Michelin's three-star category. No matter how much standards slip in Paris restaurants, and they do of course in this age of mass tourism, such an ideal of perfection remains a gastronomic keystone for a number of Parisians, including many who will never in their lives eat in a three-star restaurant.

There are innumerable cookbooks in France, as in most other countries, but in addition there is a literature of gastronomy, devoting to the pleasures of eating the same aesthetic consideration as is given to the fine arts. Jean-Anthelme de Brillat-Savarin was born in Bresse, the region in France, north-east of Lyon, which is the most renowned for food and restaurants. He was a magistrate and a minor functionary but his name lives on because he wrote the first of the classic books about eating and cooking. *La Physiologie du Goût*, the 'physiology of taste', appeared anonymously in 1825, and ends with Brillat-Savarin's famous epigram 'Dis-moi ce que tu manges, et je te dirai ce que tu es.' (Tell me what you eat and I'll tell you what you are.) At the time his recipes were thought to be divinely inspired and a whole kilometre (well over half a mile) of Paris is named after him, the Rue Brillat-Savarin in the 13th *arrondissement*.

For more than half the twentieth century, cooking in France was dominated by the name of another gastronomic writer, Auguste Escoffier. Like England's Mrs Beeton, who set the standards in the kitchen for middle-class Victorian England, Escoffier became the high priest of French cooking. His *Guide Culinaire*, published in 1902, sets out in careful detail so 'nothing would be left to chance', as he put it, how to prepare thousands of dishes in the repertoire of grand cooking. It was not until the 1960s that many professional chefs in France felt they could depart to any extent from the Escoffier bible.

Once upon a time, the Swiss produced the best watches, the Germans made the best cameras and every rich man aspired to have a French cook.

Theodore Zeldin, *The French*

Good eating in France starts long before food is cooked. When you see men and women shopping for food in Paris, you see them sniffing at melons, prodding at cheeses and earnestly discussing with shopkeepers and stallholders the freshness of vegetables and the different cuts of meat. Good ingredients are always the basis of the best French cooking, which is why Bresse and the town of Lyon in particular have such a high reputation for good food: the marvellous produce from Provence is on the doorstep. But the street and covered markets of Paris, and almost every *quartier* has one or the other, are nearly as good. *Fruits de mer*, shellfish and crayfish, at good Paris restaurants can taste as if they have just come off the boat.

The old Paris food market at Les Halles, which Emile Zola called 'the belly of Paris', was some years ago, like London's food market at Covent Garden, moved outside the city. But the new site was well chosen: food supplies for Paris now come into Rungis, right beside Orly airport so that some fresh food can be flown in and a few hours later be on sale in the street markets of Paris.

And in the Rue Saint-Antoine is the kind of heart-stirring street market which makes British visitors stand and gape and feel we are still on food rationing.
Jill Crawshaw in *The London Evening Standard*

One of the best food markets in Paris is in the Rue Mouffetard, Ernest Hemingway's 'wonderful narrow crowded market street', a long road that leads out of the Place de la Contrescarpe in the 5th *arrondissement*. Smells of enticing spices from North Africa mingle with the tangy perfume of Cavaillon melons from Provence, the fresh sea-smells of *rascasse* (scorpion fish), conger or *loup de mer* (sea bass) from the Mediterranean, musty aromas of little round goat cheeses from Sancerre, in the Loire Valley, and dozens of other piquant, savoury, fragrant, fresh, mouth-watering smells which make a slow walk along the Rue Mouffetard like eating a ten-course banquet, without putting on an ounce of weight! 'As an introduction to Paris,' John Russell believes, 'few streets are more expressive than this companionable inferno'.

Just round the corner from the cafés and bookshops of Saint-Germain-des-Prés, the stalls of the Marché de Buci crowd into the Rue de Buci and the Rue de Seine. This is the most 'literary' of Paris food markets. Writers, publishers, editors shop here alongside local housewives, shopkeepers and tourists buying fruit and cheese to eat in the little garden next to the old church of Saint-Germain-des-Prés. There is even more of a last-minute scramble here, than in most other markets, to get served before one o'clock when the stalls are closed down, some for a few hours, others for the rest of the day. All the markets of Paris close on Monday, which is why so many restaurants also close that day, because there are no fresh ingredients available, although it has also been suggested that another reason is that the top chefs, who sometimes behave like film stars, like to extend *le weekend* on their country estates.

Parisian waiters, still more often than not wearing the traditional low-cut black waistcoat, have a taciturn professionalism and put up a resistance to the friendly chit-chat you find in London, where many waiters are convivial Italians, or to the easy-going egalitarianism of New York. At all levels you can find a practised seriousness about serving food and only Paris seems to have such a collection of ordinary modest restaurants that have become institutions, as much a feature of the city as the Eiffel Tower. In these simple inexpensive restaurants almost anyone might eat, and almost everyone has eaten at some time, from the President to a film star to a rich industrialist.

One such restaurant is Le Petit Saint-Benoît at 4 Rue Saint-Benoît, which runs north from the Boulevard Saint-Germain to the Rue Jacob. It has the look of an eighteenth-century restaurant and for over 125 years has been serving good casseroles and roasts, at one time mostly to regulars whose napkins were kept in numbered slots of the mahogany cabinet that still stands in the corner. Since the 1950s three dedicated women have been running it, offering the same reliable home made dishes, made with fresh ingredients, at prices that seem like an anachronism. On a warm summer evening, the handful of tables on the terrace outside are more hotly fought over than any in the grandest restaurant in Paris.

On the other side of the Boulevard Saint-Germain, the Restaurant des Saints-Pères is on the site of an old monastery, which explains the name of the Rue des Saints-Pères alongside. There has been a restaurant here since 1850 and the same dark amber paint on the walls must have been there all that time. Three generations of the same family have been looking after customers here since 1930, still keeping the tradition of generous red and white check napkins, big enough to tie round your neck. It is hard to imagine any writer, professor or politician in Paris who has not eaten here at least once. Ask any taxi-driver anywhere in the city for the place, without giving an address, and the chances are they will know where you mean. Nothing is eternal and when one day the Restaurant des Saints-Pères puts up its shutters for the last time, Paris will not seem quite the same to a lot of people.

The busiest restaurant in Paris, which is also one of the biggest, is Chartier at 7 Rue du Faubourg Montmartre in the 9th *arrondissement*. There is little refinement here, food at the best is of middling quality but served in a true Parisian style at unbelievably low prices. For Chartier is the last surviving mid-nineteenth-century workers' *bouillon*, a kind of soup-kitchen, that somehow has lingered on, with the décor and waiters in black waistcoats and long white aprons intact. Not that Chartier is in any way a set piece arranged for tourists. This is how it has always been and this is how it goes on.

For with such old traditional restaurants in Paris, new owners may come and go, in the way that incumbents of a church change, because of death or old age, but often nothing else changes. It was Madame Fernande Allard who back in the early 1930s established the gastronomic reputation of Restaurant Allard at 41 Rue Saint-André-des-Arts in the 6th *arrondissement*, winning a precious one star in the Michelin guide for her long hours at the ovens. Her husband André, who had a gift for searching out the best wines in the vineyards of Burgundy, died in 1983 and a year or two later Fernande took a well-earned retirement. But there was no question of the new owner changing the name or anything else. The welcoming marble-topped tables remain, waiters still wear the same long cotton smocks and the same open kitchen, which any customer can look into, has been taken over by the young chef Didier Remay, who learned his art working for years by the side of Madame Allard herself. Even the most regular of regulars would not notice any difference at Restaurant Allard.

Right at the top of the list of restaurants as institutions comes La Tour d'Argent, at the top literally, since it occupies a penthouse high up on the Left Bank, just opposite the Pont de la Tournelle. It would be unfair to call the Tour d'Argent pretentious, because the food is genuinely outstanding, the wines superb and no one can remember when it did not have three stars in *Michelin*. But it is solemn and serious, as befits perhaps a temple of gastronomy, guardians of the faith of French cooking and luxury. Hemingway in *A Moveable Feast*, his reminiscences of life in Paris, recalls the Tour d'Argent's more modest days in the early 1920s, when he says they rented out a few rooms above the restaurant, offering tenants a discount on meals. Later the owner visited New York where he enjoyed the Rainbow Room at the top of the Rockefeller Center, so when he returned to Paris he moved his own restaurant up to its present rooftop level.

The Tour d'Argent used to be the most expensive restaurant in Paris. That may still be true and it is quite easy to spend there £100 a person (about $165) for dinner. But it is no longer considered to be the best. Two or three more recent restaurants are said by experts to surpass it.

Jamin, praised earlier in this chapter for what it can do with mashed potatoes, and Taillevent, between the Avenue de Friedland and the Champs-Élysées, compete with each other at the present time to offer the best meal on earth. Both restaurants, of course, have been awarded three stars by the Michelin guide. Neither is a place to look in on the spur of the moment, when you fancy say *gelée de caviar à la crème de chou-fleur* at Jamin, or *millefeuille de homard aux pointes d'asperges* at Taillevent. A table for dinner must be booked anything up to two months in advance.

From his seat in the midst of the table, the host (like a Giant in a Fairy story) beholds the kitchen, and the snow-white tables, and the profound order and silence there prevailing. Forth from the plate-glass doors issues the Banquet – the most wonderful feast ever tasted by mortal . . . **Charles Dickens** at dinner in Paris, 1856

There was a time when chefs, like judges, had to be elderly men, portly and magisterial, weighed down by indulgence and responsibilities. The new school of 'breathtaking young chefs', as one gastronomic writer calls them, are trim, lithe and athletic. Jean-Claude Lhonneur, a young chef in his early thirties, relaxed and wearing jeans, has recently taken charge of the kitchen in the cellar of Le Grand Véfour, which has the eminence of a restaurant where Napoleon Bonaparte's brass nameplate kept his corner table permanently reserved, where Victor Hugo, Sainte-Beuve, Flaubert and Balzac were regulars, where Colette used to eat nearly every day, and even when she was too ill to go there from her nearby apartment, had the daily menu sent to her for comment, and where Jean Cocteau designed the menu-card. The interior is listed as an historic monument, an authentic survivor of the Directoire style from the period of the Revolution. The setting, the most beautiful of any restaurant in Paris, is on the edge of the Palais-Royal Gardens. With all that to live up to, Jean-Claude, when you talk to him, seems boyish and calm about the awesome responsibility he has taken on of maintaining such a reputation and holding on to Le Grand Véfour's star-rating in the Michelin guide.

The younger chefs, caught up in the permissive ideas of the 1960s, have broken free from formalised culinary principles dictated by Escoffier over half a century ago and have demanded freedom to be innovative to the limits of their imagination. A new style of cooking was introduced, many would say healthier, which the influential food commentators Henry Gault and Christian Millau labelled *nouvelle cuisine*. Chefs no longer entrust the arrangement of food to waiters but arrange it themselves in the kitchen, seeking to make each plate an exquisite piece of abstract art. *Nouvelle cuisine* portions are minuscule, the price per ounce of food astronomical, but it has caught on with a society so much more conscious of health and cholesterol.

There is some doubt now whether the new trends are here to stay. The famous international chef Paul Bocuse, who was president of the *Nouvelle Cuisine Française* society, has supposedly dismissed it all as something of a joke. Others believe that the foundations laid down by Escoffier should be combined with increasingly innovative cooking. There are undoubtedly signs in some Paris restaurants of the pendulum swinging back, at least a little way.

. . . nouvelle cuisine *is getting very* vieille, *and those exquisite miniatures served up as works of art, but hardly big enough to feed the duck that donated a fraction of an intestine, have been replaced by stews that* grande-mère *once cooked.* **Kate Baillie** in *Time Out*

As in most other cities American 'fast-food' chains have established a foothold in Paris, because they are new and have an American charisma about them, especially for young people and for office workers in a hurry. But a certain veneration of food lingers on and Parisians of all classes never stop talking about it. There are more serious restaurants in Paris, because the French are more serious about food.

THE
ART OF
LIVING

Paris is a city that celebrates being alive and traffics in our desires. They call it *les douceurs de la vie*, or the pleasures of living, and one way or another in Paris, this is usually sensuous, inviting at times a hedonistic indulgence that is difficult to resist. Kenneth Clark, in his television series *Civilisation*, believed this approach to life is expressed with the utmost refinement in the wonderful series of six tapestries, called *The Lady and the Unicorn*, dating from about 1500, perfectly displayed round a circular room in the Cluny Museum near the Sorbonne. The tapestries exalt the five senses, but with such seductive beauty that it is easy to overlook that they are all about worldly pleasures, which the French organise so well.

Parisians can be conventional and set in their ways but they are not usually puritanical about enjoying anything, from food to sex. They gape in amused wonder at the distance in Britain or the United States between private pleasure and public morality. In England a sexual scandal, even in the permissive 1980s, forced a senior member of the government to resign; and then recently in America, allegations of a clandestine relationship with a model caused a contender to withdraw his candidacy for the Presidency. In Paris such matters are seen differently. If as happened not long ago, some unlucky misadventure on the way home from a nocturnal romp brings something to light about a government minister, Parisians look at the unfortunate offender not only with sympathy, but with renewed interest and admiration. They are down-to-earth about such things. When a dozen or so years after Louis XV came to the throne of France in 1715, at the age of five, he seemed rather hesitant about showing a normal interest in women, his ministers acted with dispatch. They surrounded the King with a bevy of attractive young women,

ready and willing to serve the national interest. It is not by chance that the *chaise-longue* was invented in Paris, and that later the French name for this accommodating piece of furniture had to be adopted in London, because characteristically there is no equivalent word in English.

A less demanding pleasure in Paris is simply to watch the passing show. The price of a drink on the terrace of a well-situated café, such as the Café de la Paix facing the Opéra, may seem high but it does include a ringside seat at one of the great fashion shows of the world. Self-presentation for women in Paris plays a big part in the art of living and there is no age at which they stop working at it. Paris, it is claimed, is the only city where women can be more interesting and attractive at forty-five than they are at twenty-five.

Paris . . . is wrenchingly beautiful, and so are many of its people. If you use your eyes and take in everything, you can learn more about true style and chic in a weekend than in a lifetime's perusal of fashion magazines.
Lucia van der Post in the *Financial Times*

French is a more erotic language than English and, whatever their age, there is an appealing femininity about the way attractive women living in Paris talk, dress, gesture and move. At their best, they seem to understand the essence of being a woman and to take uninhibited pleasure from it. Assistants in the grander perfumeries, such as Guerlain at 2 Place Vendôme, behave to their customers like princesses holding court and graciously dispensing distilled charm.

Chic, which may originate from nineteenth-century artists' slang, is a peculiarly French word, once again adopted by English, because there was no other way of expressing the same thing. It summons up a certain kind of attractiveness which is both self-assured and seemingly effortless. Chic can of course mean elegant and *soigné*. But some women in Paris manage to look chic in a different way, calculatedly and provocatively dishevelled, as if they have just got out of bed. It is a look that is achieved with a cleverly contrived disorder. When years ago jeans came over from America, before long Paris was cutting them in a way that turned jeans into casual high fashion.

Just as only a few people can afford to eat at three-star restaurants, so only a few rich women can hope to be dressed by the famous Paris couturiers, where a dinner gown costs anything from £2,000 upwards (nearly $3,500). But the idea is there for *all* women, of looking at the process of draping clothes over the body as a way of enhancing beauty or seduction and as a work of art. At all levels there is a passionate interest every year in what is revealed at the 'collections' of Cardin, Yves Saint-Laurent, Corrèges, Lanvin and the other top designers.

Christian Dior died in 1957 and his name remains as legendary as the name of a great painter or composer. It began with a revolution in fashion, and as in so many revolutions, Paris led the way. Christian Dior's 'new look' was unveiled to a standing ovation on the 12 February 1947. Lush femininity had returned after war-time years of austerity, as models, trained by Dior to walk and whirl with arrogant disdain, swept down the catwalk in their full skirts and padded hips. Soon afterwards a multinational fashion and beauty business spread out from Paris to London and New York and then to other cities.

Following the strict laws of elegance is . . . one of the ways of bridging the gap between oneself and everything one is not . . .
Christian Dior, from a talk given at the Sorbonne

The windows of the Dior shop, which opened in 1947 as a tiny boutique, now stretch a long way round both sides of the corner of Avenue Montaigne and the Rue François I, near the Champs-Élysées. Inside it is like a fairyland, in silver and grey, the traditional Dior colours, of luxury, fashion and style. The staff make a show of keeping up the arrogant Dior manner but slip well short of it, as it would take a queen rather than a shop assistant to match up to this Hollywood-set of an interior.

The Rue du Faubourg Saint-Honoré, which runs parallel to the Champs-Élysées, is the show place for most of the other leading couturiers. It is as statutory for them to have a window on this street as it is for the best English tailors to have an address in Savile Row or for New York theatres to be on Broadway. Coco Chanel even lived in this street among the fashion houses, not quite 'over the shop' but in a gracious house at No 39. Walking along the Faubourg Saint-Honoré is like turning

Window-dressing in the Marais

the pages of the glossiest magazine, as the Parisian flair for window-dressing takes the centre of stage. These are windows on high-living and the prices of the clothes displayed are inconsequential to the point when they are sometimes not shown.

There is more high-living further along the Faubourg, at the British Embassy, a palace which Wellington bought a year before Waterloo, as his town house in Paris. Before that it had belonged to Pauline Bonaparte, Napoleon's sister, and her sumptuous bed is still there, hung with golden curtains draped from the claws of a Napoleonic eagle, a *folie de grandeur* for any ambassador's wife who fancies sleeping in it.

Of course much of the window-dressing in other parts of Paris is as commonplace as anywhere else. But at any turn, in a road off the Boulevard Saint-Germain maybe, or in a narrow street in the Marais, a designer or an imaginative owner may offer passers-by a demonstration of the quintessential Parisian art of display. Nor does it have to be a clothes shop. A baker shop, cake shop, hardware shop or any other kind of shop might put on an inspired show. La Mère de Famille has been a confectioner at 35 Rue du Faubourg Montmartre since 1761, making on the premises a lot of what it sells. The window is a study in temptation. Homemade jams, conserves, jars of boiled sweets, crystallised fruits and other confections, undreamt of by the sweetest tooth, are lovingly arranged to look like something between a brilliant piece of pop art and a child's sweet-shop.

Paris believes it invented style and perhaps it has a case, as it puts it on the same level as art. For fashion has been given its own museum, in the most august place possible, within the precincts of the Louvre itself, the great museum that houses the Venus de Milo, paintings by Rembrandt, Raphael, Rubens and so many other masterpieces. To give the Musée des Arts de la Mode, the new costume museum, even more prestige, it was opened, on 28 January 1986, by François Mitterrand, the President of France.

The new museum, which has its entrance at 109 Rue de Rivoli, mounts temporary exhibitions with an expansive mixture of high drama and wit. The opening show·displayed nineteenth-century fashions, including bicycling bloomers in articulated action on a mechanical tandem and feathered turn-of-the-century hats, perched on a tree beside birds of paradise.

The Christian Dior memorial show, the following year, had models standing on gigantic clothes boxes 10m or so long (nearly 35ft), with the lids slightly askew and white tissue paper peeping out. On the next floor a model in a wedding-dress was flying high in mid-air over an enormous gilt-framed mirror 6m long (about 20ft), so that visitors could also see the layers of lace petticoats. But instead of everyone thinking how daring and bold it all was to have a major costume museum as part of the Louvre, there was mild surprise that it had taken so long. 'The absence of such a museum up until the present seems inexplicable!' said the Minister of Culture.

To the rest of the world, Paris has always been the capital of gaiety, good taste, pretty women, luxury and fashion . . . Everything is appearance, everything is visual.
Claude Nori, *La Photographie Française*

Eating for the French plays such a major role in the art of living that it had to have the previous chapter of this book all to itself. But that could not possibly be long enough to offer more than a few crumbs from the overflowing cornucopia of gastronomic riches in Paris. As well as restaurants, there are so many cafés to choose from for a meeting, that you can always find one that accords with the occasion. In . Saint-Germain-des-Prés, Aux Deux Magots or the Café de Flore, with all those literary associations, provide a good atmosphere to meet a publisher, your literary agent or a script editor, and meetings like that are often going on in one café or the other.

A few minutes' walk away, facing the Rue de Sèvres, Au Sauvignon, like a small crowded sitting-room, has been serving for over half a century such romantic wines as young Beaujolais and Sancerre. It is well-matched for young lovers. The wide pavement terrace of the Café de la Paix, by the Opéra, is good, as we have seen, for a free fashion show; but further inside, the gilded columns and *Belle Époque* or Edwardian décor offer a comfortable intimate setting for a more middle-aged love-affair.

La Tartine at the seamy end of the Rue de Rivoli, No 24, is the place to meet for conspiracy. This was Leon Trotsky's favourite café, before he returned to Russia in 1917, and the dim lighting from the art nouveau chandeliers, with half the lamps not work-

ing, and the friendly anonymity still make it a good place to plot and intrigue. *Tartine*, a slice of bread and butter, is an understatement as the name of this old café. The same intransigent woman behind the counter has, since time immemorial, or so it seems, been cutting generous doorsteps of excellent bread to make their famous sandwiches, which can be accompanied by one of the best choices in Paris of wine by the glass, all at cheap prices. Revolutionaries are usually both hungry and impoverished.

It is the nature of Paris to add refinement and luxury to any idea it adopts. It took the custom, at home in the vicarages of England, of tea with cucumber sandwiches, scones and butter, and turned it into discreet but determined self-indulgence in *salons de thé*, sometimes giving them the name of a real or imaginary Marquise-de-something-or-other, to add a touch of class. Gilt chairs, round marble-topped tables and a *carte des thés*, offering a choice of tea from a whole list of different blends, make up the scene. The indulgence comes from *gâteaux*, *pâtisseries* and *tartes* designed to undermine all resistance to temptation. Angelina, at 226 Rue de Rivoli, right at the other end from the proletariat La Tartine, has been famous for nearly a century for its almond-coated croissants, 'a post-coital Ritz', as *Time Out* describes it, 'where half the love-affairs of Proustian Paris began and ended.'

Tea may have been the national drink of Britain, although it is not so easy to find places in London that still serve it, but Paris has given it the professional treatment. A shop in the obscure Rue de Bourg-Tibourg in the Marais sells 250 different kinds of tea and almost as many different teapots to make it in. At teatime at the Salon de Thé Saint-Louis, there are over fifty different teas to choose from. Not that there is an accepted teatime in Paris. That would be out of character for, like British licensing hours, it would seem to the French an absurd restriction on enjoyment. Tea and indulgencies are usually served from mid-morning until well into the evening.

Unlike London, evening in Paris is not a signal for the city to move into a vespertinal mood. Instead evenings seem more like the dawning of a new day of activity, a new round of pleasures. The rush-hour goes on for longer than in most places as it is mixed up with people coming into Paris as well as people going home. Of course, as in other cities, a lot of people do go home

from work by car or train, have something to eat and then doze off in front of television sets. But *Paris* never seems to go to sleep.

I now live entirely in a suburban house, but at night from my window I see a glow in the sky. It is a reflection from la ville lumière *and gives me the happy feeling that people are enjoying themselves, as they always have and always will, in Paris.*
Diana Mosley, 'Why I love Paris' (from *The Spectator*)

Food shops and some markets are open into the evening, you can buy books or records until midnight, cafés and restaurants are lit up until late and the street lighting has a silvery incandescence about it that pushes sleep away. These are the reasons why *chansons* of the twenties called Paris *la ville lumière*, the city of light. Some of the old nightlife no longer rings true. The Folies Bergère, with its famous bar and memories of Maurice Chevalier and Mistinguett, is rather sad these days, although the spectacle is still staged with a polished professionalism. And even the famous Bluebell Girls at the Lido on the Champs-Élysées are now choreographed by a computer. The Crazy Horse Saloon, off the Champs-Élysées, has also moved into legend, even though it was only opened in 1951. Such places cling to an old innocents-abroad image of *Gay Paree*, but are now kept going by packaged tourists and bored businessmen. Even the word *gay* no longer has the same meaning.

For Parisians a night out, if it is not the cinema or a concert or the theatre, is eating out. Restaurants, such as La Coupole in the Boulevard du Montparnasse, or Boffinger the old brasserie by the Place de la Bastille, will take table bookings only up to eight o'clock, because as the evening wears on there are too many people coming in. And both restaurants welcome diners up to at least one o'clock in the morning.

La Coupole is a phenomenon as well as an institution. The food is no better than average, the noise when it is playing to a full house, which is usually about eleven o'clock at night, makes conversation impossible, the *maîtres d'hotel* and the waiters are professional but uninterested, yet the feeling of life-force, of taking part in a long-running successful show, even if only as one of the supporting cast, still gives a late dinner at La Coupole

a special quality. The playwright and lawyer John Mortimer is said to have described it as his favourite restaurant in the world, and a surprising number of people would agree. After all, it does serve nearly fifteen hundred meals a day and in the evening there is always a queue for a table.

Picasso, Dali, Hemingway, Corbusier, Giacometti, Bunuel, Andy Warhol, Joan Baez make just a random selection of the luminaries who have eaten at La Coupole, and the clientele is still brilliantly varied. Any evening there are young people on their way into life and old people on their way out, trying to enjoy what remains to them. Or a film producer is having dinner with a successful writer, with a couple of pretty young actresses for company and to help the deal along. At another table a famous pop singer is protected by black sunglasses or elder statesmen wear sober suits. La Coupole, with its banal 1920s décor, drifting haze of cigarette and cigar smoke, crowded tables and undistinguished food, still casts a spell, even if no one is quite sure why.

Inevitably there is a dark side to the pleasures of Paris at night, and not to mention this sleazy underworld would leave the picture incomplete. In the side streets of Pigalle there are so-called *life-shows*, which are no more than joyless demonstrations of copulation for sad-faced voyeurs. The *belles de nuit*, a kindly euphemism for prostitutes, are crudely blatant in the Rue Saint-Denis, a road, it is said, that in recent years has claimed the lives of two bishops through heart-attacks.

Before the night is over, some cafés are already opening up to serve strong coffee and croissants for breakfast, or a *fine à l'eau*, a brandy and water, to those in need.

Betwixt all those stars there was one only that had a special meaning for us by summoning up that aromatic bowl . . . for I can tell you that the joy of living for me was encompassed by that first hot, heady mouthful, that mixture of coffee, milk and bread – the daily gift at dawn. **Antoine de Saint-Exupéry,** *Terre des Hommes*

A new day is dawning and it is a strange paradox that in a city where there is so much emphasis on serious eating, breakfasts should be so perfunctory, although fresh croissants are available at daybreak and the coffee is usually good.

PARKS
AND
GARDENS

Right in the centre of London, the city seems to come to an end for a while and a great expanse of wooded countryside and open fields takes over, as Hyde Park spreads into Kensington Gardens. It could almost be miles out of town. Central Park in New York is a heaven-sent nineteenth-century clearing, hemmed in by a threatening metropolis. The parks in Paris are neither rolling countryside nor desperately salvaged open spaces. They are part of the landscaping of the city, in the way that French windows of a large country mansion open up on to gracious terraces, lawns and flower beds.

Londoners treat the parks in their city as their own private estates, where they are free to roam at will across the grass, boat on the lakes and sleep in deckchairs. Parisians behave more like tenants in their parks, or as if some magnanimous milord has thrown open his gardens for the day to the local peasantry. They have to mind how they go, sit on hard upright iron chairs, and if they venture on to the grass, they are ordered off at once by shrill imperious blasts from the whistle of an unsmiling park-keeper.

The parks of Paris turn out to be more like gardens, mostly formal and laid out with urban precision, gardens in a city rather than fields and woods. On the Left Bank, the largest green open space is called a *jardin*, the Luxembourg Gardens. To look at an aerial view is to see at once that these are gardens belonging to a palace, the palace built 1615–31 for Marie de Médici, widow of Henri IV. She bought the greater part of what was then a rural site on the edge of the city, from the Duke of Luxembourg, because she wanted a palace with a great park round it, like the lovely Boboli gardens round the Pitti Palace in Florence, where she had been brought up.

Time off in Luxembourg Gardens

Although the frontage of the palace was extended in the nineteenth century with two projecting wings, these are in the same style, so the exterior still reflects the purer line of classicism, free from exaggerated decoration, that the queen's architect, Salomon de Brosse, brought back into French architecture in the seventeenth century, and which might have helped Marie de Médici to feel more at home. Not that she enjoyed living there for long as six years afterwards she was exiled.

The palace is now the seat of the Senate, the upper house of the French parliament, and the gardens have an appropriate formal dignity about them. There are statues all over the place, stately enough when seen as part of the landscaping, but not to be looked at too closely as they are mostly banal nineteenth-century pieces. Yet some of the subjects make them interesting: George Sand, Stendhal, Verlaine, Flaubert among others. Walking through the Luxembourg Gardens you can feel like an intruder. At the same time they are the most popular gardens in Paris, crowded on a sunny afternoon with mothers and children or students reading their books, because the Sorbonne is not far away. Thackeray when he walked round here in 1840 found them 'melancholy, quaint old gardens' and they can still seem peculiarly private.

Only the Médici Fountain, hidden away at the end of a long pool, to the right of the palace, recalls the name of the Queen of France whom Paris has to thank for the Luxembourg Gardens. And it is right that it should be called after her, because it is Italian enough to belong to Florence. With overhanging trees and a statue of naked young lovers, Acis and Galatea, the cyclops Polyphemus looming over them, this is the most inviting and romantic corner of the Luxumbourg Gardens, a gentle retreat that attracts young lovers and old philosophers.

Although it is called a *park*, the Parc de Monceau covers little more than half the area of the Luxembourg Gardens. It is the nearest in Paris, maybe the nearest in France, to an English garden. There is a touch of English 'sweet disorder' about it, rare indeed in French landscape architecture. It was laid out towards the end of the eighteenth century, and adorned with pseudo-classical follies, some of which have survived. So there is an unexpected Roman colonnade, medieval 'ruins', a pagoda and other pieces of architectural bric-a-brac. As usual the

Love in Luxembourg Gardens

nineteenth century added to the fun with a collection of statues, languid, listless damsels stretched out at the feet of Guy de Maupassant, Gounod, Chopin, plus the odd nymph and Adonis.

The Parc de Monceau is in one of the most fashionable parts of Paris, at the end of Avenue Hoche, leading out of the Étoile, so it is a place where well-dressed middle-aged ladies gently walk off creamy *mille-feuilles* they had for tea, and bored au pairs push expensive baby carriages.

The children (one feels) are all titled, the bonnes *are visibly miracles of distinction and the babies masses of point lace; the ladies on the chairs must be Comtesses or Baronnes, and the air is carefully scented. That is the Parc Monceau.*

E. V. Lucas, *A Wanderer in Paris*

If the Parc de Monceau is genteel and well-bred, the Jardin des Plantes, the Botanical Gardens of Paris, is down-at-heel scrubland. This goes with its situation in an unfashionable out of the way part of the town, to the east near the Gare d'Austerlitz. Tourists rarely come here, so they miss out on peaceful gardens, remarkably unpretentious for Paris, with some interesting things to see, including an antiquated menagerie with llamas, bison, tigers, bears and 'peacocks . . . that look at you with silly eyes', as Henry Miller saw them. It was the menagerie that made the gardens the sensation of Paris in 1827, when the first giraffe in France arrived from Egypt, as a present to Charles X. It was fed from an upstairs window and everyone flocked to see it. Even fashions were affected for a while and spotted dresses became all the rage.

The Botanical Gardens were created a long time ago, in 1626, by Louis XIII's physicians, as the Royal Medicinal Herb Garden. In the eighteenth century they became a distinguished centre for botanical studies. It was about this time in 1734, that a cedar of Lebanon was planted on a slope overlooking the Seine, and you still hear the romantic legend that it was brought back from Syria by one of the botanists, Bernard de Jussieu, who kept it alive on the journey by potting it in his hat and feeding it some of his personal ration of drinking water. Jussieu did bring it over and plant it himself, but apparently only across the English Channel, as it was a gift from London's botanical gardens at Kew. Either way, it is worth the toil up the hill to sit on the simple stone bench, lean back against this venerable tree and make a living contact with the world of the early eighteenth century.

If the Botanical Gardens have a dilapidated charm about them, away from the mainstream, the Tuileries Gardens are majestically sited, extending for a kilometre, well over half-a-mile, between the great courtyard of the Louvre and the Place de la Concorde. They were, after all, laid as the gardens of a royal palace, although the palace is no longer there. It had been built in the mid-sixteenth century for Catherine de Médici, Queen and Regent of France, and would have occupied the area between the projecting west wings of the Louvre, where the Avenue Général Lemonnier is now.

Although the queen never lived in the palace, supposedly on

advice from her astrologer, it has played the part many times of the royal residence in the capital. Louis XVI was brought there after the Revolution and again in 1791 after he was arrested at Varennes. Later it became Napoleon's residence. After the Restoration in 1814, it was the palace of Louis XVIII, Charles X and Louis-Philippe. Last of all, in 1852, the emperor Napoleon III moved in.

To have some idea of the grandeur of the Tuileries Palace it is enough to recall that Bonaparte built, as the entrance to the courtyard, the Arc de Triomphe du Carrousel, and that for six years, 1809–15, that triumphant archway on the palace threshold bore aloft the four glorious golden horses looted from St Marks in Venice. All that remains now of all that splendour are old paintings and engravings, as the Tuileries Palace was burnt to the ground in 1871 when the second Commune, the revolutionary government, was set up in Paris. The arch was left behind with nothing to lead into but the Tuileries, the palace gardens to the west.

These look like gardens of a palace, French formal landscaping at its most aristocratic, little changed since they were laid out in the mid-seventeenth century by Le Nôtre, Louis XIV's gardener. Here there is no 'sweet disorder'; nothing is left to chance or to nature. The trees are disciplined by stern pollarding, the paths are dressed by the right and the flower beds are kept in their place.

At Paris I took an upper apartment for a few days in one of the hotels on the Rue de Rivoli; my front windows looked into the garden of the Tuileries (where the principal difference between nursemaids and the flowers seemed to be that the former were locomotive and the latter not).
Charles Dickens, *The Uncommercial Traveller*

The only plebeian touch is the name of the gardens, the *Tuileries*, after the old tileworks, which occupied the site before the palace was built, using the clay soil for making tiles, *les tuiles*.

Like most formal gardens, the Tuileries are for strolling in and enjoying the vistas. For this purpose, Le Nôtre raised two terraces, symmetrical of course, on either side. The *Terrasse du Bord de l'Eau*, alongside the Seine, is one of the most delightful

walks in Paris and yet not so many visitors come here. You walk along, in or out of the shade of the precise row of clipped lime trees, with the Seine below on one side and the Tuileries Gardens below on the other, passing the new Musée d'Orsay on the Left Bank of the river, until the terrace ends just before the graceful sweep of the Pont Royal, Louis XIV's bridge completed in 1690.

Le Nôtre's central avenue in the Tuileries gives Paris one of its splendid perspectives. Punctuated by round and octagonal ponds, it looks straight across the Place de la Concorde lining up, in true Parisian symmetry, with the three-thousand-year-old obelisk from Egypt, in the centre of the great square, to the Arc de Triomphe, at the top of the Avenue des Champs-Élysées, over three kilometres, almost exactly two miles away.

A few minutes' walk away from the Tuileries, on the other side of the Rue de Rivoli, are other royal gardens, as private and secluded as the Tuileries Gardens are public and exposed. The Palais-Royal Gardens are more like the spacious inner quadrangle of an Oxford or Cambridge college. Nor is it all that easy to find the way into them, for they also are not often visited by tourists. The palace they were laid out for is still there, although much changed, and bureaucrats have replaced the aristocrats. Men and women with brief cases and serious faces now hurry through the doorways, as the Palais-Royal is occupied by government departments.

To begin with it was not a royal palace but the *Palais Cardinal*, built in 1624 for one of the great statesmen of France, Cardinal Richelieu, first minister to Louis XIII. Richelieu's own private theatre was built into the east wing of his palace and this later became the permanent home for Molière's company. Some of his famous comedies had their opening performance here. This was the theatre where Molière collapsed on stage in 1673 and died a few hours later. For a master of dramatic irony, it was the perfect play for his last performance, *Le Malade Imaginaire*. Around the corner you can see, although not sit in, the chair in which Molière collapsed, kept as a precious theatrical relic in the upstairs foyer of the Comédie Française.

The Palais Cardinal became the Palais-Royal when a year after Richelieu died in 1642, Louis XIII died, and his queen moved in there with her son, the young Louis XIV. Not that

much of that old palace still stands, only a gallery on the side by the Rue de Valois. Most of the rest was restored in the eighteenth and nineteenth centuries.

The elegant arcades round three sides of the Palais-Royal Gardens, formed by 180 perfectly equal arches, are part of a profitable property development scheme carried out in the 1780s. By then the palace had passed to the Duke of Chartres, later the fifth Duke of Orleans. A big spender, always needing more money, he saw a chance to put his property in a fashionable part of Paris to commercial use. The arcades were built, with shops on the ground floor under them. Terraces of apartment houses were built above. The Palais-Royal Gardens became a fashionable promenade but then degenerated into the vice centre of Paris, a concentration of prostitutes, pimps and con-men. The elegant arcades were thronged with bare-bosomed women offering themselves to passers-by.

Like Speakers' Corner in Hyde Park, the gardens were also used for political speeches. One Sunday afternoon, the 12 July 1789, the revolutionary Camille Desmoulins jumped up on the table of a café and in a famous speech appealed to the crowd to take up arms. Two days later the Bastille was attacked and the French Revolution had begun.

Long since those events, the Palais-Royal Gardens have been left in peace and are now rather like the gardens of grace and favour apartments. The arcades are an elegant promenade for shopping and strolling, although not many people seem to come here any more.

Whether the weather is fine or foul, most evenings about five o'clock, I go and walk in the Palais-Royal gardens. I am the one you will see there day-dreaming alone . . . politics, love, philosophy and taste are the subjects I talk to myself about . . .
Denis Diderot, *Le Neveu de Rameau* (c.1761)

The cafés with tables under the arcades never seem crowded, yet the setting is idyllic and near one of the busiest parts of Paris. Further along, Le Grand Véfour, established over two hundred years ago, is the distinguished restaurant, where (as mentioned in an earlier chapter) Colette used to eat when she was still well enough to come down from her apartment overlooking the gar-

Modern sculpture at the Palais-Royal

dens. Altogether the Palais-Royal Gardens are an enclosed world apart, left with the ghosts of the past. Or so it seemed, until 1985. That year two fascinating pieces of modern sculpture were positioned in the Galerie d'Orléans, the double colonnade at the south side of the gardens.

These are two fountains by the artist Pol Bury. Each one has seventeen large stainless steel balls which become mobiles as the weight of the water gently turns them. The effect is calm and reflective, with enough movement to avoid monotony but not so much as to be restless. The next year the courtyard of the palace itself was dotted with an assortment of 260 black-and-white striped columns of varying heights, made out of marble from the Pyrenees. It caused an uproar in Paris when these were installed in this cherished historical setting of classical eighteenth-century architecture.

The artist is Daniel Buren who sees space and sculpture integrated to form a complete work of art. This is what he has attempted in the *Cour d'Honneur* of the Palais-Royal. He has taken over the whole space, three thousand square metres, over 3,500 square yards, with his arrangement of columns. At first sight it seems bizarre and meaningless. But the effect changes when there are people around, some sitting on the columns, children playing round them, people leaning on them. Then the courtyard is turned into living sculpture. Daniel Buren, who won the Golden Lion award for his work at the Venice Biennale of 1986 and has had an exhibition in London at the Serpentine Gallery in Hyde Park, has not claimed that this is what he intended. But this is how his columns work, in the courtyard of the Palais-Royal.

In another part of Paris is a collection of outdoor sculpture of an altogether different kind. It has been called 'the biggest accumulation of statues in the world'. You can find it at the end of the Avenue de la République which runs east for nearly two kilometres, or about a mile-and-a-quarter, out of the Place de la République. There on hilly ground is one of the largest open spaces in the city, the cemetery of Père-Lachaise. It is called neither a park nor a garden but the rows of old lime and chestnut trees, the gentle landscaping and the view over the city below make this a tranquil and nostalgic walk on a sunny Sunday morning. It is a place to get lost among shady winding paths,

Sunday morning in Père Lachaise

with romantic statues on all sides to provide 'intimations of immortality', memories of the sound of music, the words of poetry, novels and plays, and the colours of paintings. For there is nothing mute or inglorious about many of the people buried here. Père-Lachaise is a cemetery for the great and famous.

It was laid out at the beginning of the nineteenth century and named after Louis XIV's confessor, Father La Chaise, who had contributed generously to a Jesuit house of retreat on the site. At the end of the long avenue leading up from the entrance a strangely romantic tableau in stone welcomes visitors, living or dead. Bartholomé's 'Monument aux Morts' is at the foot of the hill on which the chapel stands. Surrounded by pretty maidens, a naked couple, hand in hand, are passing through an open doorway, presumably on the way to their death, although the whole thing seems erotic enough to give the impression they are going into a bedroom to make love.

The French can be morbid and highly emotional about death. They have been known to fling themselves on to graves and moan aloud in their grief. So there is nothing restrained about many of the memorials on the graves in Père-Lachaise. Chopin is buried here, in the spot he had chosen, next to his friend Bellini. Twenty years before, when he left his native Poland never to return, he had been given a silver casket full of Polish earth. This was opened at his funeral and the earth sprinkled on his grave. The statue of a sorrowing nymph guards his tomb and there is usually a bouquet of fresh flowers in her arm, all part of the life and death of one of the great romantics.

I go out but rarely but when I do take a walk,
I go to cheer myself up in Père Lachaise.
Honoré de Balzac in a letter to his sister (1819)

There is a large shrine here for Heloïse and Abelard, lovers and scholars in Paris in the twelfth century, 'whose hands sought less the book than each other's bosoms', as Peter Abelard wrote in his autobiography. Their effigies lie side by side, surrounded by iron railings, and there is sometimes a bunch of fresh flowers thrown into the enclosure. Molière lies next to La Fontaine, both beneath modest tombstones. Racine has a sombre sepulchre but not as gloomy as Delacroix's vast black casket.

Edith Piaf's simple grave is usually surrounded by fresh flowers. So is the simple tombstone of the actress Simone Signoret, who died a few years ago. Another actress, Sarah Bernhardt, flamboyant in life, is buried beneath an unexpectedly modest slab with only her name and dates engraved on it.

In different parts of the cemetery, the name *Jim* is spray-gunned on trees or tombstones, with arrows, which eventually lead to the grave of Jim Morrison, one of the pop-group *The Doors*, who died in Paris in 1971. Empty beer cans litter the area around his grave where there is always a huddle of guitar-playing followers hoping to commune with his spirit.

One of the best pieces of sculpture in Père Lachaise, and worth seeking out, is Jacob Epstein's memorial to Oscar Wilde, paid for, as the inscription records in English, 'by a lady as a

Epstein's memorial to Oscar Wilde

memorial of her admiration of the poet'. Epstein's sculpture is striking and powerful, a male attendant spirit in flight, with a marvellous sense of being airborne. The genitals were broken off some years ago, by two English ladies, it is said, who were outraged by their size. Another version is that Epstein was asked to remove them. Either way, they apparently served for some time in the cemetery office, as a paperweight.

Although the Bois de Boulogne adjoins Paris, starting a little over a kilometre, or just over half-a-mile, from the Étoile, along the broad tree-lined Avenue Foch, it is not considered part of the city itself. Most of it is unfenced and has been left as a forest, extending more than two thousand acres, on the north side as far as the Porte Maillot and on the south almost up to the banks of the Seine. Napoleon III had liked the informality of English parks during his first exile as a young man in London. When he returned to Paris, after the revolution of 1848, and became Emperor four years later, he wanted to keep the *Bois* as much like open country as possible. Perhaps for this reason the maze of paths, riding tracks and artificial lakes are reminiscent of Hyde Park.

In the spring the *Bois* is like countryside, with carpets of primroses, cowslips and wood violets covering the ground. By the summer, the Allée de Longchamp, through the wood, becomes for nearly three kilometres, almost two miles, a continuous arcade of overhanging trees.

I will not describe the Bois de Boulogne. It is simply a beautiful, cultivated, endless, wonderful wilderness.
Mark Twain, *The Innocents Abroad*

Although too many roads have been cut through, and it is no longer so easy on a hot summer's day to get away from the urban clutter of parked cars everywhere, the Bois de Boulogne is still a beautiful expanse of woodland to have so close up against the city. Enclosed within it, like a separate park, is the *Bagatelle*, and here no cars are allowed. The Bagatelle has its own secret gardens: one of the loveliest of rose gardens, a walled iris garden and another enclosed garden, with a whole wall two hundred metres or so long, about 220 ft, covered in different varieties of clematis.

In the late eighteenth century there was a fashion among the rich for follies, curious temples, illogical pagodas, *bagatelles* or mere trifles, as they were called. The future King Charles X, competing in extravagance with his sister-in-law Marie-Antoinette, wagered her that he would have a folly built during the short period of her stay at Choisy. The plans were drawn up in two days and an exquisite house was built in only sixty-four days. The prince won his wager and the *Bagatelle*, as it came to be called, is a jewel of eighteenth-century domestic architecture in the middle of the park, now named after it. It has been called 'the most ravishing folly in Europe'.

The gardens of the Palais-Royal

GRANDES PLACES AND BOULEVARDS

The Georgian squares of London are personal and intimate, with the gates often locked, the keys restricted to the owners of the houses around. Contrast the expansive grandeur of the *Place Vendôme* or the *Place des Vosges* with the cosy domesticity of some London squares, Trevor Square near Knightsbridge, for example, or Canonbury Square in Islington. In New York, Washington Square has some pretensions to elegance but has become absorbed by Greenwich Village, the 'Left Bank' of the city. As for Times Square, it is more the intersection of Broadway and 7th Avenue than a real square and was only called the 'Great White Way' because of the psychedelic glare of neon advertising signs. Paris, on the other hand, is so clearly a city of the truly *Grande Place*, lavish open squares that aerate and give such a feeling of urban spaciousness.

Whatever the final judgement of Baron Georges Haussmann's replanning of Paris in the mid-nineteenth century, there is no doubt that the broad sweep of his boulevards and wide avenues clearly lay out the arteries of the city. These swathes of anonymous uniform tree-lined highways that were cut through Paris, and which once seemed so cold and impersonal, are being reassessed now, as they seem more and more part of the style of the city, as well as helping Paris to adapt to the needs and demands of the remaining decades of this century. London has no boulevards to speak of, save the Mall, Park Lane and a stretch of the Embankment; and whilst Manhattan has its named and numbered avenues running north to south, these have nothing like the dignity and authority of those twelve great avenues radiating from the Étoile.

Spaciousness and graciousness in Paris go back long before Haussmann. An eighteenth-century achievement is there to

Place des Vosges in the Marais

look at, a breath-taking example of townscaping in the grandest manner. Great lines of poetry sometimes lose their power to astonish because they have become so familiar. Everyone knows what the Place de la Concorde looks like and in our anxiety to walk across or drive round it, through endless streams of unyielding traffic, it is easy to overlook the scale and mastery.

For André Maurois this was 'the most beautiful architectural complex on this planet'. He was a Frenchman so perhaps he was going over the top. Not that it is easy to match anywhere in any city with the Place de la Concorde. Alongside the Seine, here are the crossroads of Paris. A western gateway, formed by Coustou's superb sculpture known as the *Marly horses*, opens up on to the Champs-Élysées rising away to the Arc de Triomphe in the distance. The Tuileries and the great palace of the Louvre are to the east. The Rue Royale to the north, between two fine eighteenth-century palaces, leads to the Madeleine. And to the south, across the river by the Pont de la Concorde, built in 1791 using some of the stones from the old Bastille so that 'the populace could forever trample the ruins of the old dungeons', is the self-important portico, in the style of a Greek temple, of the old Bourbon Palace. This is now the Chambre des Députés, the French lower house of parliament.

The square was laid out 1757–72 to set off an equestrian statue of Louis XV. The architect Ange-Jacques Gabriel is commemorated by the Avenue Gabriel which runs parallel to the Champs-Élysées and leads into the square he designed. He also built the splendid façades of the two palaces on the north side, at each corner of the Rue Royale. In 1907 the palace on the left became the Crillon Hotel, perhaps the most distinguished hotel in Paris, certainly the one with the most spectacular view, right out over the Place de la Concorde.

Suites in the Crillon are furnished mostly with Louis XVI furniture from the eighteenth century, a period when French furniture was at its most elegant. The restaurant is in the sumptuous Ambassadors' Room, where in 1778 Louis XVI and Benjamin Franklin with other American representatives signed the Treaty of Friendship, recognising the independence of the thirteen states. A link with America continues, as the United States Embassy is only a little way along in the Avenue Gabriel. But the price of the marvellous view from the bedrooms in the

Crillon, over and above what it costs to stay there, is the continuous muffled roar of traffic which, in spite of double-glazing and heavy silk curtains, still intrudes.

To begin with, the square was called the *Place Louis XV*, with the statue of the king in the centre. But it was not to remain the royal square for long: during the Revolution, the statue was pulled down and the name changed to *Place de la Révolution*. The square became the scene of some of the most famous executions in history, starting with the king, himself, Louis XVI, guillotined on 22 January 1793 in the place that had been built to honour his grandfather Louis XV. Different figures are quoted for the number of people executed in the Place de la Révolution. It was many more than a thousand and included Marie-Antoinette, Madame du Barry, Charlotte Corday and then, as fear bred suspicion, leaders of the Revolution itself, Danton and Robespierre.

When the guillotine finally came down here, in 1795, a new name had to be found for the square, to exorcise the atrocities that had taken place there. *Place de la Concorde*, the square of harmony, was a good choice. Choosing a monument for the centre was also a political decision. An obelisk over three thousand years old, from the ruins of the temple at Luxor in Egypt, had been offered to Charles X in 1829 but the transport of a monument 23m or 75ft high, weighing 230 tonnes, required a considerable feat of engineering. The obelisk did not arrive in Paris until four years later, early in the reign of Louis-Philippe, in time to make a suitable non-controversial monument for the centre of the Place de la Concorde, at the same time providing a good upright against which Parisians could align their passion for symmetry.

Nobody could feel at home living in the Place de la Concorde, even with a suite at the Crillon; the scale of it is overwhelming, as it was intended to be. Further east, in the heart of the Marais district, is another *grande place*, the first one to be built in Paris, which is gracious and spacious, without seeking to dominate or impress. The Place des Vosges would be a delightful place to live, if you could afford it, in an apartment in one of the elegant thirty-six terraced houses, fronted with red brick and pale golden stone.

When you see those high windows and brick facings, divided up and framed by stone, as the splendour of the setting sun illuminates them, you feel something of the same reverence you experience in front of a state assembly, arrayed in scarlet robes, trimmed with ermine. **Gérard de Nerval** on the Place des Vosges (1854)

The Place des Vosges was extraordinarily ahead of its time when it comes to town planning and it is hard to believe that it was built as long ago as 1605–12. It was inspired by Henri IV, on the site of an old palace, but was not completed until two years into the reign of his successor Louis XIII, whose statue was erected in the centre. The *Place Royale*, as it was first called, was a great innovation for Paris, a generous open space in the middle of a city of constricted narrow streets. It is still out of place among the confined byways of the Marais, which are all around, some with their old names, such as the *Rue du Pas de la Mule*, the street of the donkey's footsteps, which leads straight into the square.

For some people, the Place des Vosges is the loveliest square in Paris, not imposing or dramatic, but harmonious and intimate, with the simplicity of true elegance. The monotony of what could have been too much uniformity is interrupted by differing shades of the brick façades, the longitudinal lines of stone tablets and the steep black-slated roofs with irregular dormer windows. The continuous arcades at ground level, now occupied by shops, galleries and cafés, add an airiness to the terraces, as well as providing a promenade in the shade and a stage for occasional jazz groups on Sunday mornings.

Like the other statues of kings in Paris, the statue of Louis XIII was toppled during the Revolution and the name of the Place Royale was changed. The *département* of Vosges in the east of France was the first to pay up its dues, to support the new government set up by the leaders of the Revolution, and in gratitude, or *pour encourager les autres*, the Place Royale became the *Place des Vosges*. The name remains today and a replacement statue of Louis XIII was put up in 1818. To look at, the square has changed so little since it was built over 350 years ago.

The best view of the square is from the windows of Victor Hugo's old apartment on the second floor of No 6, in the southeast corner, open to the public as a museum dedicated to the

writer. Such a beautiful square has inevitably attracted other distinguished residents. Richelieu lived at No 21; and at No 1, Madame de Sévigné was born in 1626, a witty and intelligent woman, whose letters to her daughter and friends have become part of French literature.

If, as suggested earlier in this book, Paris behaves as if it invented *style*, it shows it off, as if to the manner born, in another square, built nearer the end of the seventeenth century. The architecture and proportions of the Place Vendôme express aristocracy and affluence with such ease and grace that whoever we are it is easy to feel inferior as we walk into it.

It is a *grande place*, octagonal in shape, 224 by 213m, nearly 750ft across in the longest direction. This great space has been handled by the architect Jules Hardouin-Mansart with a masterly sense of proportion so that everything here feels in scale, 'more drawing-room, in fact, than parade ground', as John Russell described it.

The Place Vendôme is another square that was first conceived as a setting for the statue of a king, and in 1686 the statue of Louis XIV, Louis-le-Grand or the 'Sun-King', as he was called, was duly erected. The square was designed as a showpiece, a brilliant parade of façades, with arches below, and classical pedimented pavilions at focal points. Here again are French steeply-pitched roofs but this time the curved dormer windows are regularly placed. Nothing breaks the uniformity and the whole square ends up as an accomplished example of how harmony and perfect proportion alone can avoid any feeling of monotony and dullness. But it was all for effect: there was nothing behind the façades to begin with and nobody knew what would go there. Although work had started on the square in 1685, it was not until 1720 that the last building behind the façades was added.

Louis XIV's statue, like his father's in the Place des Vosges, was torn down during the Revolution. Then in 1810 came a real touch of imperialistic grandeur. Napoleon ordered a column to be erected, bound with a bronze spiral made from 1,200 cannons captured in the Battle of Austerlitz in 1805, with a statue of himself at the top, in the guise of Julius Caesar. There followed a game of 'musical statues'. The statue of Napoleon was replaced in 1814 by a statue of Henri IV. Louis-Philippe put back a statue

of Napoleon, but this time in contemporary uniform. The revolutionary government, proclaimed in Paris in 1871, toppled the whole column, and there is a famous dramatic photograph showing it falling down. Finally three years later, the Third Republic had it rebuilt, mounting on top a copy of the original statue of Napoleon, once more doing an impersonation of Julius Caesar. That is how it is now, the column too high for the proportions that Hardouin-Mansart intended, but time has made us rather fond of it.

These days the Place Vendôme is as expensive as it looks, with internationally-known jewellers and fashion houses under the arcades, from Cartier to Schiaparelli. There is also of course the *Hôtel Ritz*, at No 15 'a little house to which I am very proud to see my name attached', as César Ritz said when he opened it in 1898. That seems a modest understatement for a place that has welcomed guests such as Winston Churchill, Charles Chaplin, Greto Garbo and Sam Goldwyn, and that offers suites, named after the Duke of Windsor, Coco Chanel, the Prince of Wales, Scott Fitzgerald and Ernest Hemingway, complete with their own personal saunas and jacuzzis.

If the truth be known, the few ultra-sophisticated 10,000-francs-per-day [about a thousand pounds or $1,650] offered by the world's most luxurious hotel are not exorbitantly priced. The Ritz's other superbly redecorated rooms are within the price range of the average emir and Texas oil mogul.
Gault and Millau, *The Best of France* (1982)

At the end of the Rue de Rivoli to the east, the Rue Saint-Antoine takes over. It is the oldest main thoroughfare in Paris, going back to the Romans, and was given its present name in 1450. It leads into a square that sooner or later becomes known to every schoolchild in Europe, the Place de la Bastille. The *Quatorze Juillet*, the 14 July, and the name of the square at the end of the Rue Saint-Antoine continue to evoke the whole concept of human liberty in an ideological way and of the class struggle in a political sense.

Symbols are often more real than reality and the events of that day in 1789 hardly live up to the glory that surrounds the name *Bastille*. It was built 1370–82 and served for four centuries as a

fortress and a prison, mainly for men of high rank who were enemies of the king, rather like the Tower of London. Old prints show it to have been formidable and oppressive, with high walls and eight towers, 25m, or about 80ft high, an obvious symbol of power and tyranny. But well before 1789, it had already fallen into disuse and was scheduled for demolition, so there was more than a trace of farce about the famous siege on 14 July that year. There were only seven prisoners in the dungeons, down and out criminals, who were triumphantly paraded around in carts, none of them having the slightest idea of what was going on.

Anyone making a pilgrimage today to the Place de la Bastille, and people do, would find untidy bustling crossroads with popular cinemas, cafés and cut-price shops. The bronze July Column in the centre, with the figure of Liberty at the top, is not a memorial to July 1789 but in memory of Parisians killed during the uprisings in July 1830 and 1848. Lines of cobblestones at the west side of the square mark out the site of the old fortress but all that remains now are some massive stone blocks from one of its towers, discovered when the Métro was being built in 1899. These have been dumped a few minutes' walk away in the little Square Henri-Galli by the Pont de Sully.

Even for the *Fête Nationale* on the 14 July each year, the bandstand erected in the Place de la Bastille is a modest affair, more appropriate to a square in a small provincial town. But the busy old square, with all its sentiment and history, will be given new life and interest when the new Bastille Opera House opens in 1989, the bicentenary of the storming of the Bastille.

As well as the *grandes places* of Paris, there are some charming small squares, tucked away and often unknown to visitors. *Vert Galant*, the debonair cavalier, you could say, was the sobriquet for Henri IV, one of the most popular of the kings of France during his reign, 1589–1610. And it is a fitting nickname for a king who enjoyed riding his horse down the corridors of the Louvre and making love to a whole string of attractive young women. His statue stands in the middle of the Pont Neuf, the oldest bridge in the city, and behind it a flight of steps leads down to the Square du Vert Gallant, on the very tip of the Ile de la Cité. It is a quiet garden square with a perfect view of the Pont Neuf and the river, as romantic a spot as the king it is named after.

Henri IV, who gave Paris the lovely Place des Vosges, also left behind a smaller square, in its own way just as delightful. The Place Dauphine, named after the son of Henri IV, is on the other side of the Pont Neuf, opposite the Square du Vert Gallant. Although it is usually lined with parked cars, there is no through traffic and this quiet triangle, with men playing *boules* in the middle, seems as remote and peaceful as a village square, except that the men and women sitting on the terraces of the cafés, sipping glasses of wine, are more lively and well-dressed. André Breton described the Place Dauphine as 'one of the most profoundly secluded places I know'. Even the vast neo-classical front of the Palais de Justice, that dominates the east side, is screened to some extent by a row of young chestnut trees.

Nothing ever seems to happen in the tiny Place de Furstenberg. It is another world from the hectic life of Saint-Germain-des-Prés, just around the corner. People sit on the benches in the shade of the old paulownia trees, the old-fashioned lamp-posts with their white globes look as if they are gas-lit, which they are not, and an occasional tourist passes through looking for the entrance to Delacroix's old studio at No 6, in the corner of the square. That is about all, except when yet another film unit discovers this peaceful *place* and realises that it is the perfect location for shooting a film about old Paris.

It is so strange, this square place *with its ten trees correctly aligned, its intimate and exact proportions . . . When a taxi crosses the Place de Furstenberg, you wonder what on earth it is doing there.*
Daniel Halévy, *Pays Parisiens*

For more animation, there is the friendly Place de Passy, the one-time village square in this now fashionable district in the west of Paris. Café tables, under colourful umbrellas, spread out all round the small square, and at lunchtime there is the intermittent thump-thump-thump of a waiter chopping up *baguettes* with a hinged knife. Paris, which can provide some of the most sophisticated pleasures in the world, is also good at offering the simple life, like having lunch in the sunshine at one or other of the two welcoming cafés in the Place de Passy.

The wide avenues and boulevards in Paris belong mostly to the wholesale replanning of the city in the second half of the

Place de Furstenberg

nineteenth century. But the widest and the grandest of them all was started centuries earlier. Although it looks like spectacular town-planning, the Avenue des Champs-Élysées did not come about in that way at all. It began as a piece of landscaping to open up a distant prospect. Le Nôtre, Louis XIV's gardener, who laid out the Tuileries Gardens in the 1670s, extended the vista by planting rows of chestnut trees, and the area was called the Champs-Élysées, the Elysian Fields. About half a century later, the Director of the Royal Gardens extended the avenue of trees to the top of the hill in the distance. When that was completed in the 1720s, the Avenue des Champs-Élysées ran its complete course as it does now, from the Place de la Concorde to the Étoile, although it would have been hardly more than a rough thoroughfare through undeveloped land.

There is nothing elysian about the Champs-Élysées today, as anyone knows who has tramped wearily along it, although its great width and the vistas in both directions still impress. It has become one of the commercial streets of the world, with airline offices, shops, cafés and a permanent motor show, since Fiat, Volvo, Renault, as well as other car manufacturers, have their glossy gleaming showrooms on one side or the other.

This long, wide, tree-lined avenue, with the Arc de Triomphe at the top and so many vantage points for television cameras, is a gift to any president or general for field-days, marching along at the head of any procession that comes to hand. General de Gaulle made the most of it, as he would, when he entered Paris on 25 August 1944, German snipers still around, and held his victory parade along the full length of the Champs-Élysées, then on to Notre-Dame. It was one of the greatest moments in the history of France.

London, it has been said, has long preferred decent plumbing to grandeur. New York is a *showbiz* city that goes all out for magical glitter. Paris has the unmistakable look of an imperial city. The monuments are so magniloquent, like the Arc de Triomphe and the ponderous solemnity of Napoleon's tomb in Les Invalides. The vistas are so arrogantly pre-eminent, like the outlook from the terrace of the Palais de Chaillot, across all those fountains, perfectly lined up with the Pont d'Iéna over the Seine, leading to the Eiffel Tower and the great expanse of the Champ de Mars, with the École Militaire in the far distance.

Napoleon I introduced imperialism. It is not by chance that his statue on the top of the column in the Place Vendôme shows him as Julius Caesar, for he had a vision of the French empire as equal in glory to ancient Rome. On 2 December 1804, only fifteen years after the Revolution, he was proclaimed emperor, impatiently snatching the crown from the Pope, in front of the high altar of Notre-Dame, and crowning himself. No French king ever identified himself with Paris in the way that Napoleon did. 'The Emperor wishes his capital,' he declared, 'to have an appearance in keeping with its illustrious destiny.' So he built triumphant arches and planned majestic public buildings.

The houses I demolished to make way for the Carrousel and the
Louvre cost another seventeen million. I did vast things. But what
I was planning to do, that was something altogether in another
class! **Napoleon I**

His nephew, Napoleon III, who became emperor in 1852, the last sovereign in France, had the same ambitions for Paris. And funds were available, as this was an era of economic expansion and industrial growth. Railways were being built, new businesses developing. In 1853, Napoleon appointed Baron Haussmann as his chief commissioner for Paris, with the briefing that 'We must make every effort to make this great city more beautiful. We must build new avenues and make the dark, airless, crowded slums healthier places to live in.'

Under Haussmann's direction, from 1853–70, the narrow crowded streets were replaced by broad tree-lined avenues and boulevards, fronted by stone-faced buildings six or seven storeys high. The Étoile, or the Place Charles-de-Gaulle, to give its new name, still seldom used by Parisians, was replanned and seven new avenues were splayed out from it like spokes from a huge wheel. The Boulevard de Sébastopol was driven through the centre of the Right Bank from north to south, the Opéra was built and given its own wide avenue leading up to it. Paris became the city of boulevards and *boulevardiers*.

The prettiest women to stare at! Here I touch on a weakness in the
life of Paris which there is no doubt the Boulevards have fostered.

Staring – more than staring, a cool cynical appraisement – is one of the privileges which the Boulevardier most prizes.

E. V. Lucas, *A Wanderer in Paris*

Paris lost much of its medieval picturesque charm as Haussmann's boulevards and avenues ripped through the old districts. A walk through the confined streets of the Marais, left largely untouched, such as the Rue Charlot, the Rue Sainte-Croix-de-la-Bretonnerie, the Rue des Rosiers, where the pavements are so narrow that two people cannot walk side by side, leaves an impression of what most of Paris would have been like.

Henry James, who loved Paris, complained of 'The deadly monotony . . . that Haussmann called into being, its huge, blank, pompous, featureless sameness.' But even James found it difficult not to be impressed by the new vistas opened up and found the new avenues a great convenience. Haussmann was a vandal in some ways, destroying much that was beautiful. But he can also be seen as a visionary, although an insensitive one, with some foresight of what a city should become in the twentieth century. It is possible that without him, Paris might have been left behind as a museum of a city, in the way that Venice is.

THE SEINE – A RIVER FOR LOVERS

Different cities relate to their rivers in different ways. The Thames divides London and for Londoners living north of the river, the south side is often quite unfamiliar. The Hudson and East rivers separate Manhattan from the other boroughs of New York. But the *Seine* acts as a highway through the centre of Paris, like the Grand Canal in Venice, holding the Right Bank and the Left Bank in easy equilibrium. When Parisians talk about the *Rive Droite* and the *Rive Gauche* it is merely to indicate direction, not different parts of their city. So it is natural that numbering of houses in the streets of Paris always starts from the end nearer the river, and when streets are in line with it, the numbers go downstream.

Parisians love their river tenderly and are at home with it, many of them criss-crossing it, not just in the morning to go to work and in the evening to go home, but several times a day. And they stroll across it casually because, as visitors soon find out, the Seine in the centre of Paris is much less than half the width of the Thames at Waterloo Bridge, much less than a quarter of the long hike across Brooklyn Bridge. Only a few steps can take you from the Ile de la Cité or the Ile Saint-Louis to the 'mainland'.

Nor is the Seine in Paris so much of a mercantile river, like the Thames in the City of London. Boats can, in fact, tie up by the river, right in the centre of Paris at the Gare de l'Arsenal, a marina that starts almost at the southern edge of the Place de la Bastille. This links up via a long underground canal with the Saint-Martin's Canal, just a little to the east of the Place de la République, which in turn joins the Ourcq Canal flowing into the river Marne to the east. So a steady traffic of barges, tugboats and yachts finds its way into the Seine and prevents it becoming

purely ornamental. But when you are in the city, it is easy to see that its river serves Paris and Parisians much more than maritime trade. People take their dogs for a walk along the river banks, use the waterside on hot days for sunbathing; and tramps are at home sleeping under the bridges or getting drunk sitting on the benches.

Napoleon I loved the Seine and gave Paris a four kilometre (or two-and-a-half-miles) stretch of quays on either side, all the way round the curve of the river from the Pont d'Austerlitz, downstream to beyond the Pont d'Iéna. This has almost eliminated any danger to the city from severe flooding. Paris soon took over the new quays, using them not merely as riverside routes but for the life of the city. They filled them with hotels, cafés, shops of all kinds, from art galleries and august antique shops to a famous department store with a curious name. A pump, supplying water for the Louvre, under one of the arches of the Pont Neuf, was decorated with a statue of the Woman of Samaria, giving Jesus water at the well. It became known as the *Samaritaine*, and the name was taken for a small shop, opened at the northern end of the bridge, which was to become one of the biggest department stores in Paris.

You can stay in a hotel by the Seine, have all your meals at restaurants by the Seine, do most of your shopping by the Seine, and, without leaving the river, visit so many of the renowned places in Paris. If you took away the great buildings by the river, Paris would no longer be Paris. The Eiffel Tower would go. So would the Museum of Modern Art in the Palais de Tokyo and the vast Museum of the Louvre. The spectacular new Musée d'Orsay would vanish, and with it the Assemblée Nationale (the French parliament), the Hôtel de Ville (the town hall of Paris), the Hôtel Dieu, the oldest hospital in the city, whose foundation goes back to the seventh century, the radiant Sainte-Chapelle, the Place de la Concorde, the regal dome of Richelieu's Institut de France and even Notre-Dame. They are all by the river.

The Seine is the great romantic river of the world, where entwined lovers on the river banks and on the bridges are part of the scene night and day and seem to harmonise with the mood of the river itself, just as they might seem as out of place by the Thames as they would on Brooklyn Bridge. Whatever the consequences, it is magical and disturbing to fall in love anywhere,

A river for lovers

but Paris both invites and illuminates the experience. Perhaps that is what James Joyce meant when he wrote that Paris is 'a lamp for lovers hung in the wood of the world'. A walk along the Seine at any time of the day in any season of the year demonstrates how much it still attracts lovers, as it has done for centuries.

At night, places like the Ile St-Louis are magical. Restaurants spill on to cobbled pavements overlooking the river banks of the Seine and the Cathedral of Notre-Dame is floodlit and bewitching in the silence and dark.

James Burstall in *The London Standard*

There are two stone heads and a memorial tablet over the doorway of No 9 in the Quai aux Fleurs, near where the Ile de la Cité is linked by a short bridge to the Ile Saint-Louis. They mark the site of the house where the most famous of all lovers by the Seine, as star-crossed as Romeo and Juliet, made passionate love to each other. A certain canon of Notre-Dame lived there and his beautiful and intelligent niece, Héloïse, who was seventeen, was tutored by Abelard, an outstanding scholastic philosopher and theologian, more than twenty years older than she was. Here they became clandestine lovers. When Héloïse found she was pregnant, they were married in secret. As a revenge, Abelard suffered castration, after which he became a monk. Héloïse, forever faithful to her lover, entered a convent.

The story of their love for each other, in that house by the Seine, where 'nothing in the nature of love-making was not tried by us in our passion', emerges with so much frankness in the letters between them, written in the most elegant Latin. In the years after Héloïse became a nun, Abelard wrote over a hundred love poems for her. His autobiography, the *Historia Calamitatum*, keeps their relationship alive for us, as we read of their tender love and sexual excitement. At moments it has something of the flavour of a *Kamasutra*, written in medieval Latin.

In 1843 another famous literary love-affair began by the Seine. That year Charles Baudelaire, a poet deeply affected by the symbolism of the flowing river, moved into a small apartment on the top floor of the Hôtel de Lauzun at No 17 Quai d'Anjou, on the north side of the Ile Saint-Louis.

Beudelaire was only twenty-one and had recently returned from a long sea voyage round the Cape of Good Hope, where he had found the dark-skinned women attractive. It is recounted that as he was looking down on the Seine from his apartment, he saw bathing naked in the river a beautiful half-caste girl. That was the beginning of his long and stormy love-affair with Jeanne Duval, his 'black Venus', as he called her. He had just come into an inheritance from his father, so was able to set her up in a tiny apartment, nearby on the Ile Saint-Louis. Their love-affair inspired his collection of poems under the title *Les Fleurs du mal*, translated earlier in this book as 'the fruits of evil'. Published in 1857, it is a strange sequence of poems. Some of them are deeply disturbing in their sordid revelations. Others are idealistic, moving in their insight into the transcendent power of love.

Not many street-vendors have such a beautiful and romantic location as the *bouquinistes* of Paris, the second-hand bookstalls along the quays, mostly by the river around Notre-Dame and along the Quai d'Orsay. At one time these were places for antiquarian book-collectors, where it was possible to find an occasional rare first edition or even a manuscript. Some of the stall-holders, taking advantage perhaps of the amatory associations of the river flowing by in the background, also sold the kind of sexually explicit books that were banned in other countries. For many years before 1960, when Penguin Books successfully defended at the Old Bailey in London their right to publish the original version of *Lady Chatterley's Lover*, these friendly open bookstalls by the Seine were among the few places where D. H. Lawrence's novel could be bought, with all the words he used in it.

The Seine is a river of light; the Thames is a river of twilight. The Seine is gay; the Thames is sombre . . . the Seine has a mile of old book and curiosity stalls, whereas the Thames has nothing . . .
E. V. Lucas, *A Wanderer in Paris*

The history of Paris begins, not merely by the Seine, but in the middle of it, on the Ile de la Cité. 'That splendid capital,' wrote Gibbon in *The Decline and Fall of the Roman Empire*, 'which now embraces an ample territory on either side of the Seine, was originally confined to the small island in the midst of the river,

from whence the inhabitants derived a supply of pure and salubrious water.' Even the name itself, *Paris*, comes from that island, because the inhabitants were one of the Gallic tribes called the Parisii, who had settled there in the third century BC. But to begin with they called it *Lutetia*, a Celtic name that signifies a habitation surrounded by water. It was not until the fourth century AD that the name of the early inhabitants became the name of the city. So unlike the name London, which derives from the Roman *Londonium*, Paris is a name that belongs to France, to a tiny island in the middle of the Seine.

For a long time the history of Paris, even the history of France, you could say,was the history of the Ile de la Cité. This was all there was of Paris, even three centuries after the Parisii first settled there. This was the city that Caesar's legions found when they came to conquer it in 52 BC. The Romans built their own fortifications on the island and a temple, where Notre-Dame now stands. Two thousand years later visitors to Paris still find that the Ile de la Cité is the heart of the city. Notre-Dame, the cathedral of Paris, stands on the island, so does the Palais de Justice, the senior law courts of France, and the Préfecture de Police, the Scotland Yard of Paris. These are all on the same small island, entirely surrounded by the waters of the Seine. The very coat of arms of Paris acknowledges the city's debt to its river: the centre of it dominated by the emblem of an ancient sailing boat.

The Ile de la Cité has often been compared to a ship, because it is shaped like one, with a pointed prow, formed by the grassy Square du Vert Galant, and a curved stern. It seems to tow behind it a smaller vessel, the Ile Saint-Louis, a mere 75m, about 250ft away. If the Ile de la Cité, with its solemn buildings, is a ship of state, then the Ile Saint-Louis is a kind of pleasure-steamer. You visit the Ile de la Cité to do business at the law courts or at the Préfecture, or to light a candle in Notre-Dame, and not much happens on that island after dark. You visit the Ile Saint-Louis to queue up for the best ice-cream in Paris or for Alsatian *sauerkraut* and an earthenware stein of beer at the busy bustling Brasserie de l'Ile Saint-Louis, or for an evening out at one of the other thirty or so restaurants that find a place on this small island.

The island takes its name from Louis IX, who became King

of France in 1226 at the age of twelve and, during his long reign of forty-four years, brought to France unprecedented prosperity and peace. He lived a life of piety and ascetism, going icognito into the city to wash the feet of the poor, and some years after his death he was canonised.

As you cross to the Ile Saint-Louis it feels almost like leaving Paris behind, for the island has kept a remoteness about it. There is a village atmosphere, with narrow streets and mostly small personal shops. So far none of the big supermarkets have opened up there, it has kept off the bus-routes, nor has it found a place for a Métro station. Even now, when the island has begun to cater more for tourists, it is easier to feel an intruder here than in any other part of Paris. The noise of traffic becomes more distant and the locals let themselves through noble doorways into private courtyards beyond.

The Ile Saint-Louis was not developed until the seventeenth century and most of the buildings belong to that period, so it has an unusual unity of architecture. The river front is full of rows of 'stately old mansions', as George du Maurier called them in *Peter Ibbetson*. A walk round the quays, circumnavigating the island, is an architectural experience and one of the best ways to come to terms with how Paris relates to its river. The Pont Marie is the natural point of departure as it was built in the early seventeenth century, to give access to the island just at the time when it was becoming a fashionable place to live. Although it is a beautiful bridge of mellow stone and graceful piers, the Pont Marie is disappointingly not named after a woman. Christophe Marie designed it and rather unusually they called the bridge after him.

The engraved stone tablets on the houses along the Quai d'Anjou, to the left from the Pont Marie, are a guide to who has lived here. No 17 is the Hôtel de Lauzun where, from an upstairs window, Baudelaire saw his 'black Venus' swimming in the Seine below. This has long been a house of creative activity: Wagner lived here for a while, also the German lyric poet Rainer Maria Rilke, and the English painter Walter Sickert who, influenced by the French impressionists, painted intimate scenes in a very different setting, the drab district of Camden Town in London.

The outside of the Hôtel de Lauzun, although well propor-

tioned, is plain. Only the gilded balconies and the drainpipes, decorated with fish scales picked out in gold, give any hint of how richly the interior is decorated. The house now belongs to the city, so it can be visited at certain times. Walking round it, there is not a moment when the eyes can rest, as everywhere the walls and ceilings are covered with murals and elaborate baroque mouldings. Here is a real taste of what high living and big spending were like in the seventeenth century.

Further along the quay, at No 9, Honoré Daumier lived from 1846–63. He was a friend of Baudelaire, Balzac, Delacroix and Corot, and an exceptional caricaturist as well as a painter. A contemporary said that one of his satirical sketches illuminated a political issue 'better than a thousand newspaper articles'. The tablet outside No 7 tells us that it was built in 1642 for a prosperous iron merchant and taken over in 1843 by the Guild of Master Bakers, as a dignified mansion for bakers of Parisian *baguettes* to hold their meetings.

No 3 Quai d'Anjou, almost by now at the eastern end of the Ile Saint-Louis, near the Pont de Sully, is the Hôtel Lambert, worth pausing to look at, as it is such a gracious town house. Louis Le Vau, First Architect to Louis XIV, designed it in 1640, so we might know what to expect, as he was also responsible for a major part of the Palace of Versailles, for long thought of as the supreme example in Europe of royal splendour. This house was the setting of another tempestuous love-affair by the Seine, the explosive relationship between Voltaire and Madame du Châtelet. Chopin's impassioned piano playing would have made the perfect musical accompaniment to an affair like that one, but Chopin, of course, was not on the scene until the next century, which is when he gave private recitals of his music in the same house, in the 1840s.

Rounding the Ile Saint-Louis to the south, along the Quai de Béthune, the flying buttresses of Notre-Dame come into view. Through doorways along the quay are more tantalising glimpses of hidden courtyards and private inner worlds. The marvellous carvings of lions' heads on the wooden doorway of No 24 make these some of the finest doors in Paris. Passing No 36, we read that in 1912, the year after she received a second Nobel Prize for her work on radium, Marie Curie moved into that house and lived there for over twenty years, until she died in 1934.

The Rue Saint-Louis-en-L'Ile is the only main street on the island, like the one high street in a village. Two of the shops along it usually have queues outside. Haupois is a minute baker shop, always crowded, because they bake, in their wood-fired ovens, some of the best *baguettes* in town. And all summer there are queues outside the shop at No 31, for one of thirty or so different flavours of ice-cream. This is Berthillon, an institution known to every Parisian, many of whom cross Paris to make a pilgrimage here. It is designated by at least one responsible guidebook as 'one of the best ice-cream shops in Europe'.

There are more than thirty bridges across the Seine on its course through Paris, about twice as many as the number of bridges crossing the Thames in the main part of London. Many Paris bridges are promenades, as much for walking along as for driving across. The sedate Michelin guide to Paris sprinkles three stars, to signify 'highly recommended', more liberally perhaps for views from bridges than for anything else. Some bridges, such as the Pont Marie, at one time had houses on them or, like the Pont Neuf, were permanent fairgrounds for trades-men. One wide bridge was built just as a footbridge, on which no wheeled traffic was allowed, in order that members of the academies comprising the Institut de France, and students at the École des Beaux-Arts, both on the Left Bank, could cross the Seine straight into the Louvre, then newly established as a museum, to look at the works of art that Napoleon I had brought back as loot from his conquests. This bridge was called the *Passerelle des Arts*, the footbridge of the arts, and that name is still used, even on some modern maps. Most people know it as the *Pont des Arts*.

The Pont des Arts, opened in 1803, was the first footbridge in Paris in modern times. Even though a toll was charged, it is recorded that sixty-five thousand Parisians walked across it on the opening day. In the last few years the bridge has been com-pletely rebuilt, following the design of the old bridge. It is a most generous footbridge, wide and handsome, with rows of seats all the way along in the middle, facing in both directions. The alignment is perfect, on the Right Bank with the fountain in the centre of the great Cour Carrée of the Louvre, and on the Left Bank with the centre of the dignified portal directly under the dome of the Institut de France.

Nancy Mitford began, what she called in *The Blessing*, 'the most beautiful walk in the world' by crossing the Pont des Arts from the Left Bank. Kenneth Clark chose for his first sentence, in the opening programme of the television series *Civilisation*, 'I am standing on the Pont des Arts in Paris.'

I am standing on the Pont des Arts in Paris . . . on this bridge how many pilgrims from America, from Henry James downwards, have paused and breathed in the aroma of a long-established culture, and felt themselves to be at the very centre of civilisation.
Kenneth Clark, *Civilisation*

Kenneth Clark was looking upstream, towards the Ile de la Cité, with the towers and spire of Notre-Dame just visible. The view downstream, from the other side of the bridge, also spells out civilisation, perhaps in even larger letters. Looking in that direction, over on the Right Bank the Tuileries Gardens impose order and form on nature to create the most urbane of landscapes. On the Left Bank, on the Quai Malaquais, are the high railings of the École des Beaux-Arts, a forcing ground since the early nineteenth century for some of the best French painters.

A little further downstream, we can see the full length of the Quai Voltaire. Voltaire, as near as you might find to the embodiment of civilisation in one man, died on 30 May 1778 at No 27. Upstream, nearer the Pont des Arts, the Hôtel du Quai Voltaire is at No 19. On the wall of the charming sitting-room is a photograph of Wagner and a letter from Baudelaire. They both lived and worked there, and so did Sibelius and Oscar Wilde. Delacroix and Corot had a studio at No 13. Ingres lived next door at No 11 for a while, when he was professor at the nearby École des Beaux-Arts. At No 9, Anatole France's father had a bookshop and this is where the novelist, who wrote such elegant classical French, lived during his early years. If as Kenneth Clark felt, civilisation is an awareness of the body and spirit, 'outside the day-to-day struggle for existence and the night-to-night struggle with fear', the view from the Pont des Arts is as good a place to come to terms with it, as anywhere in the western world.

The first bridge upstream from the Pont des Arts is the Pont Neuf. It is the oldest bridge in Paris, although its name, the 'new

bridge', has stuck to it, ever since it was completed in 1606, when it was the new bridge in Paris. It is the same story as New College, one of the oldest colleges in Oxford. The Pont Neuf is a beautiful bridge, strong and assured, gracefully crossing the river at its widest point in the city. And it is a delightful bridge to walk across, since right from the beginning it was built for leisure as well as for traffic. The pavements are generous and over every pier there are wide bays with stone seats.

If the Pont Neuf has elegance, the Pont Alexandre III goes in for excess. It is not so much as not knowing where to stop but not stopping at all. Cupids, birds, lions, wreaths, garlands, nymphs, art nouveau lamps jostle each other all the way across the river. The Belle Époque in France, like the Edwardian period in England, was loaded with confidence. Prosperity, at least for the well-off, was here to stay, or so everyone believed. Life was good, the world a playground, and the World Exhibition of 1900 was held in Paris to prove it. The Pont Alexandre III was one of the show-offs. At the time, the Franco-Russian Alliance was being celebrated and France wanted to please her new friends, so the bridge was named after Tsar Alexander III who had died a few years earlier. His son Tsar Nicolas II came in person on 7 October 1896 to lay the foundation stone. In our time, when nuclear warheads are counted anxiously by both sides, the Pont Alexandre III seems 'horse-and-buggy' stuff. But it is still there as one of the more exotic riverside attractions of Paris.

A short way downstream from the Eiffel Tower, it is possible to walk along in the middle of the Seine for 850m, that is well over half-a-mile. Many Parisians do not know about this. Not all writers of guidebooks have heard of it. It is almost unknown to tourists. And it has a pretty name, the *Allée des Cygnes*, the swans' pathway. In effect, it is a long artificial island that was built up from the riverbed in 1825 by the Pont de Grenelle Company. It is 11m, or over 35ft wide, and runs in the centre of the river between two bridges, the Pont de Grenelle and the Pont de Bir-Hakeim. In the summer it becomes a continuous arcade, all the way along, formed by overhanging lime trees, poplars and chestnut trees. At every step there are changing vistas of the river and if you are walking upstream, the Eiffel Tower is in constant view.

There are of course many other viewpoints of the Seine in Paris. One of them is a spectacular view downstream, with a host of grimacing gargoyles for company, from the roof of the south tower of Notre-Dame. But it is a hard climb up. An easier way is to take the lift to the roof terrace of the department store Samaritaine, and look out over the Pont Neuf and the Left Bank. Some people believe that the best view is downstream from the middle of Pont de Sully, with the river curving away round the Ile Saint-Louis under the beautiful Pont Marie. Lord Clark chose the view from the Pont des Arts.

With a passport and a little trouble, it is possible to get up to the Mazarine Library in the Institut de France, one of the most elegant of reading rooms, in the centre of the French literary and intellectual Establishment. From there the windows provide a scholarly peaceful view over the river, to the Louvre on the opposite bank. For the price of a Métro ticket, there is a brief but exciting high-flying view over the Seine, as the train leaves the Métro at Bir-Hakeim to fly up into the air across the river for a dizzy twenty seconds, balanced on an old elevated railway higher than all the bridges, and arrives at Passy on the other side.

LANDMARKS

It is not by chance that the renowned symbol of London is a huge grandfather clock, since the paternal chimes of Big Ben seem to echo the steadfast character of London itself. Even though it is no longer the highest building in the world, the Empire State Building still remains the primary symbol of New York, especially for people who have never been there, just as above all else, the vast elongated hollow pyramid of the Eiffel Tower means *Paris*, again perhaps more for people who have not been there.

Once you have been to Paris, it is usually *Notre-Dame*, the great cathedral in the heart of the city, that becomes for many visitors their first point of orientation. For the French themselves, Notre-Dame is the eternal centre of France, even for some the true centre of civilisation, as we know it, and in a real sense the centre of Paris. Ever since a decree issued in 1768, all distances to Paris, from anywhere else, are officially calculated to a small brass star set in one of the flagstones of the terrace in front of Notre-Dame. The centre of this modest roundel of brass is given an awesome name. It is called *Point Zéro*. From here, everything starts.

Notre-Dame arouses our respect and reverence, whereas the Eiffel Tower brings out our sentimentality and affection, and is usually the first thing we look for as our *Airbus* circles round, before coming in to land. Is any other name as commemorated as Alexandre Gustave Eiffel? His tower reaches far beyond the limits of the 7th *arrondissement* in Paris, where it stands. The French writer Roland Barthes warns us that, wherever you are in Paris, even when it is misty, 'you must take endless precautions . . . *not* to see the Eiffel Tower'. At night-time it is even more inescapable. It used to be floodlit in the usual way but

recently someone had the clever idea of lighting it from within so that at every turn the structure stands out, a radiant pyramid of light.

Nor is the Eiffel Tower confined to Paris, or even to France. Souvenir plastic replicas of it are on shelves and mantlepieces in countless rooms in countless homes all over the world. Reproductions of it, on teacloths, dry dishes in kitchens everywhere, and jiggle provocatively on T-shirts stretched over women's breasts from Tel Aviv to Tokyo. What a memorial to the name of one man! And it happened by chance.

The tower was intended to be temporary, to stand for only a decade or two, so no one bothered much about the name. Otherwise they might have called it the *Tour de la Révolution*, since it was built as part of the Paris World Fair of 1889, to celebrate the centenary of the storming of the Bastille. At the time Queen Victoria, as well as some other crowned heads of Europe, were not amused by this anti-monarchist display and refused to honour the fair with their presence. The Eiffel Tower was the tallest structure the world had ever seen, so it might have been known as the *Grande Tour*. Even the *Tour Prince de Galles* could have been run up on the flag-pole: the tower was officially opened by Edward VII, when he was Prince of Wales.

But nobody knew the show would run for ever, so the name did not seem all that important. Even in 1910, the tower's future was still uncertain and E. V. Lucas in his guide to Paris, published that year, was able to write 'How long the Eiffel Tower is to stand I cannot say, but I for one shall feel sorry and bereft when he ceases to straddle over Paris.' In the end the tower was saved by radio-telegraphy, as it was so useful for antennae, which have since increased its original height from a characteristically French precision of 300m (984ft) to an arbitrary 320.85m (1,051ft). So the Eiffel Tower was saved, although it is incredible that it had to wait until 1964 before it was officially classified as a national monument.

Gustave Eiffel must have enjoyed the reprieve of his tower, as he lived on until 1923, aged ninety-one. He deserved to get some pleasure from his work because he had suffered so much from critics. So much has been said about the Eiffel Tower, for and against. To begin with it was all against, and while it was being built it was referred to as 'that hideous column of riveted

metal' and a 'blot on the face of Paris'. Much later on, Marcel Brion called it 'a series of giant ladders for spiders with a craze for climbing'. Jean Cocteau, a brilliant designer himself, went overboard the other way, by calling it the 'Notre-Dame of the *Rive Gauche*'.

The Eiffel Tower is the big 'coach parties welcome' attraction of Paris, vulgarised by tourist shops, snack-bars and 'chips with everything' cafés. It is a sightseeing bore. Yet when the light is good and the tourists fade into the distance, Gustave's tower still seems a daring and poised masterpiece of design and engineering, a proud landmark in the technical drive forward of the nineteenth century. In England, Isambard Brunel had already shown with his suspension bridges how iron could add beauty to utility. Joseph Paxton had already built in Hyde Park, for the Great Exhibition of 1851, the Crystal Palace, a wondrous structure of cast iron and glass. The Eiffel Tower went beyond. Here was iron being used, not to copy classical columns and capitals, but as open architecture, with all its nuts and bolts and rivets on display.

A base of four metal arches gently curves inwards to thrust upwards into the sky as a single lattice column, all without a trace of traditional decorative covering of stone, marble or glass. Of all the statistics solemnly paraded about the Eiffel Tower, one stands out as the greatest tribute to Eiffel's engineering genius. The total weight, estimated as 7,000 tonnes, ends up on the ground as a dead weight per square inch of only fifty-seven pounds, or four kilograms per square centimetre, no more, it is calculated, than the pressure on the legs of an armchair, with an average man sitting in it. This is achieved by dispersing the load: the area between the bases of the arches is more than two acres.

The engineering achievement is beyond question. After all, the tower is still standing almost a hundred years after it was erected. What is less expected is that so many painters, Pissarro, Dufy, Utrillo and others, have admired its beauty. Robert Delaunay, in the 1920s, used its form for a whole series of exuberant paintings as experiments in the abstract qualities of colour. The Eiffel Tower has turned out to be the most successful publicity gimmick in history, far more effective as a piece of public relations, than anything ever dreamt up by admen in London or on Madison Avenue.

The Cathedral of Notre-Dame never seems diminished by tourism. In the Place du Parvis, the big courtyard in front of the cathedral, polyglot groups assemble, guided tours are regimented, cameras click compulsively, but in the end it is commercialised tourism that is trivialised by Notre-Dame and not the other way round. In spite of everything that has been written about it, no matter how many times we have seen it, the impact remains, the power of this cathedral to jolt us into transcending, for a few moments, the day to day matter-of-factness of our lives. It seems older than time, although we know it is not, and there are older churches and far older temples in the world. We know its history, yet it remains a mystery.

Where Notre-Dame stands on the Ile de la Cité has been a place of worship for two thousands years, since the Romans built a temple there. Archaeologists have uncovered, while excavations were going on to build a car park under the courtyard, fragments of a Merovingian cathedral that stood on this site. Later, a Norman church, or *Romanesque* as the French call it, stood here and Notre-Dame was built to replace it. The actual date when building started is not recorded. It was in the second half of the twelfth century, as we know it was conceived by the bishop of the diocese, Maurice de Sully, who was elected in 1160. The cathedral the bishop planned was to a great extent finished a hundred years later. By that time, the latter part of the thirteenth century, the familiar west front, facing the big square where tourists now gather, would have looked in form and proportion the way it does now, although the effect would have been much more colourful, because at that period statues were polychromic. But the three portals were there, with the serenely grave sculptures in the arches above the doorways, much as we see them now, because these at least have largely escaped restoration. It is this marvellous west front that, for some people, is the purest of all Gothic architecture.

Just visible upstream is the Cathedral of Notre-Dame – not perhaps the most lovable of cathedrals, but the most rigorously intellectual façade in the whole of Gothic art.
Kenneth Clark, *Civilisation*

The doorway on the right is the Portal of Saint Anne, according to tradition the mother of Mary. The tympanum above the doors contains the oldest statues in the cathedral, carved in the twelfth century, even before the portal was built. The Virgin and Child in the centre, so simple and direct in feeling, is altogether different from the sculpture of the same subject in the central column of the doorway on the opposite side, which is modern, and looks it. This left-hand doorway is the Portal of the Virgin. The grand doorway in the centre, higher and wider than the others, is the Portal of the Last Judgement.

Above the three portals is the Kings' Gallery, a parade of twenty-eight statues of the kings of Judea and Israel, as forebears of Christ. These are all nineteenth-century reconstructions and are touched by sentimentality. Twenty-one of the original heads were found recently, in 1977, not far away in foundations where they had been hidden for safe-keeping during the Revolution. These are some of the most precious treasures of the Cluny Museum and although they are mutilated and crumbling, there remains a profound impression of detached compassion.

The great rose window, almost 9m, or 30ft across, is in the centre over the Kings' Gallery. The glass may be nineteenth-century restoration but the fine tracery is as it was left by master stonemasons in the thirteenth century. Such was the quality of their work that nothing has moved out of true. At the next level up, the beautiful tracery of an open screen runs along the full width of the façade, and in dramatic contrast to this stone lacework, those massive majestic bell-towers rise up.

That is the west façade of Notre-Dame, still little different from the way Bishop Maurice de Sully planned it in the twelfth century. You could say it is the first movement of that 'vast symphony in stone', as Victor Hugo called the cathedral in *The Hunchback of Notre-Dame*.

Everyone who has ever written about Paris has to write about the superb flying buttresses that support the walls of the apse, at the east end of the cathedral. These continue to astonish us and there are people who say that every time they see them, their spirits are lifted by their lightness and grace. They belong to the fourteenth century, 1318–44, and remain a marvel in the effortless way they do their work.

The enigma of Notre-Dame is that it continues to move and affect us, in spite of all the changes it has suffered. The Revolution did a lot of damage, because it was anti-clerical as well as anti-royalist. Many of the statues and carvings were destroyed, Notre-Dame was turned into a Temple of Reason, a ballet-dancer enthroned on the high altar, statues of Voltaire and Rousseau replaced saints in their niches. The uprisings of 1830 and 1831 destroyed still more and by that time Notre-Dame was under threat of demolition. Victor Hugo's *The Hunchback of Notre-Dame* helped to save it.

A major scheme of restoration started in 1841, with Eugène Viollet-le-Duc in charge. He was an archaeologist as well as an architect, who had made a long study of Gothic architecture. Perhaps he knew too much. And it was the nineteenth century, when restorers often did not know where to stop. Viollet-le-Duc laboured twenty-three years over his work, aiming to restore Notre-Dame to his own vision of the Gothic masterpiece it had been in the fourteenth century. There was wholesale replacing of statues, including the twenty-eight along the Kings' Gallery on the west front. He added the slender spire, to offset the massiveness of the towers and because early engravings showed that a spire had been there at one time. But Viollet-le-Duc's spire lacks the spareness and simplicity of the original. Then, in what he believed to be true medieval feeling, he added all those grotesque gargoyles, jutting out everywhere.

The essential spirit and quality of Notre-Dame has somehow survived all that has happened to it and it stands there, still strangely moving and inspiring. In architecture, proportion is all, the handling of space and mass. Notre-Dame is the last of the great cathedrals in what is usually regarded as the first period of Gothic architecture and shows more assurance in the application of the new architectural principles. More light and air are let in, the arrangement of porches and windows more lucid and free, lightness and an impression of weightlessness replace the solemn heaviness of earlier centuries. The effect is to turn from meditative awe of the mystery of faith to a celebration of God. Mahatma Gandhi felt this, when he said about Notre-Dame, 'the men that made such things must have had the love of God in their hearts'.

Gothic architecture was to become more joyous and

ornamented in the centuries to come. Because Notre-Dame is more restrained, it has kept a serenity and mystery of its own. And perhaps the *Point Zéro* belongs in front of that perfect west front, purified to such a direct simplicity that it seems to say to us 'In the beginning was the Word, and the Word was with God . . .' From here, everything starts.

It would take a lot of religious fervour to find anything numinous or mystical about the Madeleine. This mammoth church is the dominant landmark in one of the most fashionable parts of Paris, at the crossroads of boulevards, just to the north of the Place de la Concorde. It is like a Greek temple that has been over-restored, regardless of expense or taste. And its history is one long architectural farce.

Building had started in 1764 by one architect, Contant d'Ivry. A second architect took over and started all over again. All work came to a standstill during the Revolution. Then in 1806, Napoleon sent orders from Poland for it to be turned into a Temple of Glory to the *Grande Armée*, where odes would be read and orations delivered on the nobility of French warriors. Many designs were submitted and Napoleon, perfectly in character, chose the most imperial of them all, a plan to erect an extravagant pastiche of the Greek Parthenon, here in the centre of Paris. Time stumbled on. Napoleon suffered defeat, monarchy was temporarily restored. At last the Madeleine was completed under Louis-Philippe and was consecrated in 1842.

While all this was going on, all sorts of other uses had been considered for the site and the half-finished building. A library was one possibility, the stock exchange another, and then even an opera house, a railway station or a bank. With its monumental flight of steps leading up to an impressive parade of fifty-two Corinthian columns, 20m, nearly 75ft high, the Madeleine could be taken for the Bank of France. In fact, it has become the society church of Paris, where the most fashionable weddings take place, that long flight of steps providing an upstage background for bridal photographs.

The Madeleine was much admired when it was built in the nineteenth century because it resembled a bank more than a church. It was a monument to worldliness, keeping a proper distance from the original Madeleine's washing of a preacher's dusty feet.
John Berger in *The Guardian*

The distinguished place to be buried is in one of the gloomy cells in the crypt of the Panthéon, although you have to warrant a state funeral. The dome of St Paul's Cathedral in London comes into view at any turn, when you are walking through the City or crossing bridges, such as Waterloo Bridge or Blackfriars Bridge. It is the same on the Left Bank in Paris, with the commanding dome of the Panthéon. You keep seeing it. Christopher Wren's dome, the first in London, and Jacques-Germain Soufflot's dome on the Panthéon both reflect a return to classical forms in architecture, influenced by the Renaissance churches of Italy. Seen from afar, they have something in common. Both have noble proportions. But St Paul's is a warm welcoming church: the Panthéon is cold and forbidding.

The Panthéon was completed about a hundred years after St Paul's, as Louis XV's thanksgiving for his recovery from an illness. The king himself laid the foundation stone in 1764. It is such a prominent landmark because it stands on a hill, the Montagne Sainte-Geneviève, and the church was consecrated as the Église Sainte-Geneviève, dedicated to the patron saint of Paris. The Revolution was to change that, turning the building into a mausoleum for the famous. The windows were blocked up, which left the interior dark and gloomy.

Twice over the next century it reverted to the role of a church. But when Victor Hugo was buried there in 1885, after an enormous state funeral, the church of Sainte-Geneviève was defrocked for the last time, to remain ever after as the Panthéon. Voltaire, Rousseau and Emile Zola are among the great and famous who are buried here.

In the end, the Panthéon makes a fitting burial place, for with its grave free-standing portico, it follows the lines of the Roman Pantheon. Even the dome has a severity about it, not as rounded and generous as Wren's dome on St Paul's. There may be things to admire about the Panthéon but there is nothing to love.

Another fine dome makes a familiar landmark on the Left Bank. This one is gold-ribbed and handsome, not at all sombre like the Panthéon. Visitors to Paris often ask what happens there, because it does look impressive. The dome covers the hall of the Institut de France, the official repository of French wisdom and enlightenment. And it looks the part. Set well back from the quay, on the opposite bank to the Louvre, with a fine

Pont Louis-Philippe and Pont Marie

colonnaded portico flanked by low concave pavilions, the whole arrangement is classical and quietly dignified. Silhouetted against the setting sun, it makes a fair sight. 'This', wrote Emile Zola reverently, 'is Paris going to sleep in her glory.'

The Palais de l'Institut, or simply the *Institut*, as Parisians call it, was completed in 1667, as a college endowed by Cardinal Mazarin, Richelieu's successor as first minister of France. During the Revolution a group of learned academies were grouped together to form the Institut de France and in 1806, Napoleon decreed that they should hold their deliberations beneath the dome of this college. The senior body is the most prestigious society in France, the Académie Française, limited to forty members, a doggedly exclusive club for men, until 1980 when a woman novelist, Marguerite Yourcenar, was allowed in. But that still left out in the cold Simone de Beauvoir who, ironically, wrote about the domination of society by men, in her manifesto *The Second Sex*, and another brilliant writer, Marguerite Duras, who wrote the scenario for *Hiroshima Mon Amour*.

For many years academicians were notable for their obscurity and it was almost a mark of distinction to be refused admission, because you would then be in the company of Descartes, Pascal, Balzac, Maupassant, Proust and other masters who were rejected. This century things have improved a little. Jean Cocteau was elected and even other film directors, René Clair and Marcel Pagnol. André Roussin, who wrote *The Little Hut*, a clever sexy comedy that ran for years in London and on Broadway, is also a member of the Académie Française, the society that turned down Molière.

If you stand on the Right Bank, looking straight across the gilded Pont Alexandre III, you see beyond a wide green esplanade and precisely in line with the centre of the bridge, the most beautiful dome in Paris, truly comparable with the sublime dome of St Paul's Cathedral, which was being built at exactly the same time. From this distance, the dome appears to sit over the centre of a very long low building. In fact it belongs to the church just behind, called after the dome itself, the *Église du Dôme*. Directly beneath the dome are the remains of Napoleon Bonaparte, entombed in a series of six coffins and finally contained in a great sarcophagus of red porphyry, the most honoured tomb in France.

Notre-Dame through the Pont de l'Archevêché

The long building is, of course, Les Invalides, built as a home for invalid old soldiers. Over six thousand were lodged there at one time. Louis XIV founded it in 1670 as a royal hostel and by 1674 the first pensioners were already in residence. There is a disciplined military order about this terrace facing towards the Seine. It is nearly 200m, or about 650ft long and the only indulgences are the droll dormer windows in the roof-space, which are encased in stone suits of armour. The façade seems to be planned to set off the triumphant central archway. The whole has a simple nobility about it, in striking contrast to the approach over the pretentious Pont Alexandre III.

The only old soldiers there now are custodians and caretakers, because Les Invalides is used for military museums and for the imperial tomb of Napoleon, which is the big tourist attraction. Surprisingly few visitors go round the back to look at the Église du Dôme. They miss the exquisitely perfect façade designed by Jules Hardouin-Mansart. Unlike most churches, the dome is mounted directly over the colonnaded front, which serves as a pedestal, so that the façade and dome appear as a simple unity in the same plane. The effect is the rare experience of flawless harmony.

Napoleon's tomb lies in the circular crypt designed by Louis Visconti, who also designed the tomb. Rue Visconti, the narrow street mentioned earlier in this book because Balzac set up his printing press there, is named after him. The tomb Visconti designed is in the grandest style, which is the way Napoleon lived. It is stately and imposing, a tomb for an emperor, and all around it are carved the names of his victories: Wagram, Friedland, Iéna, Austerlitz, Rivoli . . .

The names of those victories appear again, engraved on shields round the top of the Arc de Triomphe. Even for Paris this is a massive piece of imperial pomp. It is said to be the largest archway in the world, 50m, about 165ft high and 45m, about 150ft wide. When you are flying over the city, it stands out as much as the Eiffel Tower, not only because of its size but because of its position at the centre of a vast roundabout, the junction of twelve wide undeviating avenues. From the air it looks like a star, as the avenues radiate from the centre, which is why, of course, it was called the *Étoile*. When Charles de Gaulle died in 1970, the Council of Paris, changed the name. But the

old name is pretty, and *Place Charles-de-Gaulle* is awkward to say, so taxi-drivers and many other people as well still call it the *Étoile*.

For Napoleon, if it were big, it was beautiful. He was a great showman and Paris was his stage. Chateaubriand said of him that his favourite part was the role of Napoleon, and his favourite audience, the citizens of Paris. The Arc de Triomphe was his own idea as a monument to his victories and the brief was that 'the monument must be colossal in size'. The result is grandiose and theatrical. Work started in 1806 and the foundation stone was laid on 15 August that year, Napoleon's birthday. Building seemed to go on for ever and the triumphal arch was not unveiled until 1836, after the monarchy had been restored for the time being, with Louis-Philippe on the throne.

Fate and circumstances kept the Arc de Triomphe as a stage set for focal points in Napoleon's life, even though he never saw it completed. When he married the nineteen-year-old Princess Marie-Louise of Austria in 1810, the new empress had to enter Paris through Napoleon's arch. But the walls were still only a few metres high. So a full-scale dummy archway was erected on the site, using scaffolding covered in painted canvas. Five years later, in 1815, after the Battle of Waterloo, the route taken as Napoleon went into exile was along the Champs-Élysées, passing in front of his arch, where building had come to a standstill. In 1840, the funeral cortège, bringing the emperor's body back from St Helena, stopped under the great archway, at last completed, while a salvo of twenty-one guns was fired.

Parisians nowadays hardly look at the Arc de Triomphe, except when they watch on television the annual service for the dead of the two World Wars, for now under the arch, the eternal flame of remembrance burns. At other times they are too busy negotiating the traffic at one of the most demanding roundabouts in the world. Tourists can now avoid the hair-raising dash across to get to it, by taking the pedestrian underpass opened about twenty years ago from the north side of the Champs-Élysées.

The Sacré-Coeur basilica is in its way as theatrical as the Arc de Triomphe. It is like a badly-researched set for an old-style Hollywood musical about Arabian Nights. The style is pretentiously called *Romano-Byzantine*. This is revealed as a huge

pseudo-Byzantine edifice with five ill-proportioned minaret-like domes. The Château-Landon stone it is made from has a cold lifeless pallor and is the kind of stone that instead of mellowing, becomes whiter and more pallid with age. There were many architectural aberrations in nineteenth-century Europe and this is one of them. Yet the Sacré-Coeur is often chosen for travel posters and one popular guidebook sees it as possessing 'stunning impact and beauty'. Many critics would disagree.

Suddenly the street opens wide its jaws and there, like a still white dream, like a dream embedded in stone, the Sacré-Coeur rises up. A late afternoon and the heavy whiteness of it is stifling. A heavy, somnolent whiteness, like the belly of a jaded woman.
Henry Miller, *Black Spring*

The Sacré-Coeur stands high up on the hill of Montmartre, so it has a way of unexpectedly coming into view, wherever you are in Paris. You see it from the train as you come in from the north, up side streets from east-to-west boulevards and even when you are walking in the Luxembourg Gardens. Building was started in 1875, as a symbol of hope after the Franco-Prussian War of 1870–1, when Paris came under siege and surrendered. It was completed just before World War I but had to wait until 1919 before it was consecrated.

Many people from all over the world visit the Sacré-Coeur and walking up one of the long parallel flights of steps to enter the church does feel like going on a pilgrimage. If for nothing else, it is worth it for the marvellous view over Paris from the terrace at the top. Within the church there is a respectful reverence, as for more than half a century continuous worship before the high altar has been sustained, without a single break, twenty-four hours every day.

Seen from afar, especially at night when it is floodlit, the Sacré-Coeur can look romantic and exotic. In the end, whatever we think of it, familiarity has endeared it to us.

The Tour Montparnasse, the new tower block by the Gare Montparnasse, will never become endearing. Nor does it come into view unexpectedly. It is always there, offending the skyline of Paris, a skyscraper from Manhattan that came to be built in the wrong city. It is black and monolithic, 200m, over 650ft

high, and when it was opened in 1973, it was the tallest office building in Europe. Express lifts take coach parties up to the fifty-sixth floor. The view from the top is spectacular, looking out, on a fine day, twenty-five miles or more over the Ile-de-France. But for many people this has so much less reality and meaning than walking in the streets. For Paris is a personal intimate city, a city that becomes more rewarding the more you get to know it. And to get to know someone, you have to be close to them.

SECRET PARIS

The Pompidou Centre claims to attract seven million visitors a year, more than twice as many as the Eiffel Tower; dozens of international tourist coaches line up every day at Notre-Dame; there are usually queues to get into the Picasso Museum; at the new Musée d'Orsay you have to push your way through crowds to see the impressionist paintings. Yet alongside these attractions are other places in Paris, less known, some not covered by guidebooks, where you can take your time and be almost alone.

Not only are there museums, but narrow streets, hidden away gardens and precincts, full of character and interest, which you can explore on your own, eat at a simple café and feel you have stumbled across somewhere not everyone knows about. A few of these places are real discoveries, unknown even to entrenched Parisians. Others are listed and acknowledged but so over-shadowed by marvellous new museums and famous buildings, that only a trickle of visitors find their way to them. They offer exceptional delights and pleasures, plus a rare bonus, when all around there is so much conveyor-belt tourism, of being quiet and uncrowded.

The crowds visiting the Museum of Modern Art in the Pompidou Centre are often unaware that there is another first-class collection of modern art in Paris. The Musée d'Art Moderne de la Ville de Paris contains the outstanding twentieth-century paintings belonging to the City of Paris; and the building itself is as much a part of the history of modern architecture, as the Pompidou Centre. The collection is in the Palais de Tokyo, between the Avenue du Président Wilson and the Seine, which was built for the World Exhibition in Paris of 1937. This is 'brave new world' architecture of the 1930s, which at the time seemed so much the shape of things to come and now seems as curiously out of touch as 1930s' Buicks and Chryslers.

The first room in the Palais de Tokyo has only one painting in it, which wraps round all four walls and is referred to as the largest painting in the world, 60m by 10m, about 200ft by 35ft. You have to walk round to look at it, like following the sequence of a strip cartoon, which accords well with the style. It is by Raoul Dufy, who worked with Matisse and Braque, and then developed his own personal style of witty painting, with cartoon-like characters. His giant painting was commissioned by the Paris Electricity Board, for the Palace of Light at the 1937 exhibition, where it was given what now seems the charmingly naive title, 'La Fée Électricité', the Good Fairy Electricity. It is a vast panorama of the progress of science in the service of mankind, moving from Archimedes to Alexander Graham Bell and beyond, innocent and full of hope, because it stops a long way short of the sinister applications of nuclear physics.

Among other paintings by Dufy in the museum is 'Races at Epsom', an animated view by a French painter of horse-racing on Epsom Downs. The whole collection here ranges right across twentieth-century art. There is one of the fairy-tale fantasies of Marc Chagall, who made his home in Paris in 1910, arriving from a small provincial ghetto in Russia, adopted French nationality and lived on into the 1980s when he was nearly a hundred. We can see Montmartre at the end of the nineteenth century, through Utrillo's beautifully composed affectionate pictures of the narrow cobbled streets, which include his painting of 12 Rue Cortot, where he had his studio. Paintings by Braque and Picasso show them exploring cubism in the first decade of our own century. Robert Delaunay uses the form of the Eiffel Tower for one of the brilliant experiments in abstract colour that he did in the 1920s.

This spacious airy museum, usually quiet with not many people about, has a striking setting for an inexpensive lunch. Outside the friendly cafeteria there are tables on the terrace, which looks across through 1930s-style columns, to trees and the Seine, with the Eiffel Tower beyond. And to keep you in touch with twentieth-century art, the black-and-white panels on the chairs have a touch of Mondrian about them!

There are paintings by Claude Monet in the impressionist collection on the upper level of the Musée d'Orsay. But you can see a much greater collection, without being jostled by crowds, in

the Marmottan Museum, way out on the west side of Paris by the Bois de Boulogne. No 2 Louis-Boilly in the 16th *arrondissement* was the home of an art historian and collector, Paul Marmottan. The setting is peaceful, beside the Ranelagh Gardens, which look like an English common, with grass you can walk across and old chestnut trees left to take their own shape instead of being cut back in the usual French manner.

There was already a fine collection here of Monets and other impressionist art and this was added to by Claude Monet's son Michel, who donated in 1965 a further sixty-five of his father's paintings. This is a museum you can walk round unhurried, sometimes finding yourself alone in a room, and enjoy more than 160 of Monet's loving poems in light and colour. Many were painted in his garden at Giverny: water-lilies, the subject he so often returned to, a field of yellow irises, an arched Japanese bridge . . . On the lower ground floor are paintings for Londoners: his painting of the Houses of Parliament against the setting sun with the Thames motley-coloured in the foreground, a half sketch, half painting of Charing Cross Bridge and a delicate pastel of the old Waterloo Bridge.

Other than Monet's home at Giverny in Normandy, about 80 kilometres, or 50 miles north-west of Paris, where he lived for so many years, between 1883 and 1926, there is no better place than the Marmottan Museum to make a relationship with Monet himself. As well as the collection of his paintings, this a treasure house of personal things. You can read letters he wrote from Giverny, see his clay pipe, his small round gold-rimmed spectacles and, of course, his pallette. There is also a gentle portrait of Monet as a young man, by his friend Renoir.

One historic painting in the collection has been missing since the daring robbery in 1985. It is a glowing impression of a sunrise reflected in rippling water. Monet called it 'Impression: Soleil levant'. When it was shown at the first impressionist exhibition in 1874, a journalist latched on to the title to ridicule the whole exhibition. These are not artists, he wrote, merely 'impressionists'. Monet, Camille Pissarro, Renoir, Cézanne and the other painters in the group later came to accept the name as an apt way of describing their approach. Monet's painting of a sunrise became part of the history of art. But no one knows where it is now.

There are marvellous paintings by Monet in the Musée d'Orsay and the collection in the Marmottan Museum is outstanding. But the most sensational Monets are somewhere else in Paris. If you stroll along the Tuileries Gardens, on the side by the Seine, walking towards the Place de la Concorde, you reach a pleasant pavilion, the *Orangerie*. It was built in the midnineteenth century, at the time of the Second Empire under Napoleon III. Right on the corner of the hectic Place de la Concorde, one of the busiest and noisiest places in Paris, there is a secret world here, quiet, with rarely more than a dozen or so visitors, and given over to a contemplative art-experience.

Down in the basement are two extraordinary oval rooms, where you can imagine yourself walking round Monet's garden at Giverny. You are surrounded by a continuous sweep of colour and light formed by the purples, pinks, blues and greens of water-lilies. They are painted on huge panels set into the gently curving walls, so they become like murals encompassing the whole room. Monet offered these paintings to George Clemenceau, the prime minister who led France to victory in World War I. 'This is nothing much,' wrote Monet, 'but it is the only way I can join in the victory.' It is an unforgettable experience to be in this place, and you might easily find yourself alone there, sharing Monet's sense of wonder at the mystery of colour and light.

Monet painted the life-force of the world, as he related to it himself . . . the sun setting over the dried reeds of winter marshland, where enchanting spring flowers are reborn, in the unfathomable mystery of eternal renewal. **Georges Clemenceau**

On the two floors above in the Orangerie is a personal collection of paintings acquired by two collectors, Paul Guillaume and Jean Walter, not as investments but simply because they responded to them. Cézannes, Renoirs, Picassos, Soutines are hung almost casually in small sitting-rooms.

Paris is rich in artists' studios that have been preserved as shrines to the painters and sculptors who worked there. With the exception of the Rodin Museum, described in the second chapter of this book, these places are not on the tourist beat and are usually deserted havens with quiet intimate gardens.

Saint-Germain-des-Prés is lively, stimulating, noisy and crowded, but five minutes' walk away, not all that easy to find, is the quiet Place de Furstenberg, with benches and old-fashioned lamps. The modest doorway of No 6 in the corner leads into a simple courtyard. As we cross it, Paris seems a long way off, the noise of traffic reduced to a distant murmur, punctuated by occasional police-car sirens. At the far side a shabby staircase leads up to the apartment where Eugène Delacroix lived for the last five years of his life, now a simple museum. You walk down a stairway to the peaceful garden where Delacroix had his last studio built, supervising every detail himself. 'I like my studio,' he wrote in a letter, when it was finished in 1857, 'and I am now working there.' It still has the atmosphere of an artist's workshop, with a large skylight in the high ceiling. Delacroix was a passionate painter of religious themes and moved here so that he could be nearer to the church of Saint-Sulpice, on the other side of the Boulevard Saint-Germain, where he was painting the ceiling and frescoes in a side chapel. Vincent van Gogh, who was so much influenced by him, once said that 'only Rembrandt and Delacroix could paint the face of Christ'.

The major paintings by Delacroix are in the Louvre and other museums, but his studio and garden off the Place de Furstenberg are the best place to make a personal contact with one of the greatest French romantics, who put feeling and imagination far ahead of intellectual knowledge and technique.

Gustave Moreau was a weird painter who lived in a reclusive private world of his own, although in the last years of his life he emerged to become a professor at the École des Beaux-Arts. His paintings are so supernatural that they interested Salvador Dali and some of the earlier surrealists of the 1920s. The only place where you can see a collection of them is in Moreau's own studio just beyond the southern fringe of Montmartre, at 14 Rue de la Rochefoucauld. He lived and worked here most of his life and when he died in 1898 he left it with all the contents, to be kept as a permanent museum. The rooms are stuffed with thousands of paranormal paintings and drawings. What adds to the strangeness of visiting this place is that you may find yourself alone here, in the disturbing inner-world of Blake-like visions and madness. Even the spiral staircase, curving up into Moreau's vast studio, is fantastical.

It is often difficult to be married to a painter, even more to a sculptor, because their works take up so much more room. Antoine Bourdelle's old studio, where he worked for forty-five years, is full of monumental pieces, some on temporary exhibit, which overflow into the courtyards and garden. It is in the unfashionable 15th *arrondissement*, in a road now named after the sculptor himself, 16 Rue Antoine-Bourdelle. Bourdelle became an assistant to Rodin in 1896, working for a few years in the master's own studio. For nearly twenty years after Bourdelle's death in 1929, his wife and daughter kept his studio much as he had left it and in 1948 they offered it to the City of Paris as a permanent museum, a quiet oasis near Montparnasse.

Most guidebooks are unaware of Ossip Zadkine's studio at 100bis Rue d'Assas, by the Luxembourg Gardens. It is unknown even to many people living in the area, hidden as it is at the back of a courtyard, with a narrow entrance between two modern blocks of apartments. Since Zadkine died in 1967 it has belonged to the City of Paris and is a delightful and personal place to visit. Zadkine's accordion is on a shelf, his dungarees hang up next to his sculpting tools, pieces of his sculpture in the small garden are just as he arranged them himself.

Ossip Zadkine left Smolensk in Russia to study in London but when he arrived in Paris in 1909 he knew immediately that this was his artistic home. Cubism was on the scene and Zadkine was drawn to Chagall, Modigliani, Picasso and other artists experimenting in new ways of expressing themselves. He was one of the first to adapt the angular shapes of cubism to sculpture but moved on to express his own individual and imaginative apprehension of the world around him. His small studio is charming and deserted, and the sensitive pieces of his sculpture we see there explain why so many sculptors came to Paris from all over the world to study with him.

Bourdelle and Zadkine had both studied at the École des Beaux-Arts, the legendary art school in Paris. The words themselves, *beaux-arts*, have a ring to them that leaves the English equivalent, 'fine arts', academic and restrained. The Paris art school goes back to 1648, when the Academy of Painting and Sculpture was founded. For many years the school had space in the Louvre and it was not until the beginning of the nineteenth century that it moved across the river to the Left Bank. It now

occupies a marvellous site, a whole block between No 14 Rue Bonaparte, near Saint-Germain-des-Prés, all the way down to the Seine, by the Pont des Arts, which leads over the river straight to the masterpieces in the Louvre.

The forbidding high walls in the Rue Bonaparte make entering the École des Beaux-Arts seem difficult for outsiders, although it is often possible to walk in and mingle with the students, who provide an unrehearsed fashion show in colourful free-expression. The great inner courtyard, covered with an arched glass roof, was built 1871–4 and is now used for exhibition space. In the grounds of the school it is easy to get lost, walking through passages, cloisters and gardens, passing chipped, head-less, armless statues. It is all like an untidy run-down artists' colony, with a deserted charm and peeling paint.

With its light and elegant fabric, its pretty fountain, its archway of the Renaissance, and fragments of sculpture, you can hardly see, on a fine day, a place more riant *and pleasing.*
Thackeray on the École des Beaux-Arts,
The Paris Sketch Book, 1840

For those who hesitate to venture inside, there is a view over the wall of the art school, if you can manage to get a table by the window on the first floor of the Restaurant des Beaux-Arts, on the other side of the Rue Bonaparte. This cheap cheerful bustling restaurant has been feeding hungry students for more years than anyone can remember. It is one of the celebrated student restaurants of the world. The tables are so small and close together, you could be eating off a chessboard; but what more could you expect when you are getting a pleasant three-course meal, including a carafe of wine, for less than 50 francs, about £5 or $8? The owners of the old restaurant have changed from time to time over the long years but everything else re-mains remarkably unchanged, because no one would want to or dare to change it.

The next road up from the restaurant is the Rue Visconti, one of the narrow streets that Baron Haussmann never got round to developing. We have already noted that it is named after Louis Visconti, who designed Napoleon's tomb in Les Invalides and the florid monument to Molière near the Comédie-Française.

The Horses of Apollo

Hardly any visitors bother to walk down here, except for the few with inside knowledge. Not many cars drive along it for fear of getting blocked: it is a two-way road with not enough room for two cars to pass. Ordinary though it seems, the Rue Visconti should not be underestimated. A plaque reminds us that it was at No 17 that Balzac's printing business ran him heavily into debt, between 1826–8, and sent him back to writing. Two floors up in the same building, about ten years later, Delacroix had his studio, where George Sand waited while Chopin's portrait was being painted. We can see that famous romantic study by Delacroix in the Louvre.

On the other side of the road at No 24, there is a simple one-storey house with a blue door, where Racine lived for some years and died, it is recorded outside, on the 21 April 1699. His plays were produced by Molière in the theatre at the Palais-Royal. Further down the narrow street, a picture framer is at work, women are sewing in small workshops, a gallery owner is arranging sculpture for a private exhibition. This is Paris of the Parisians, Paris without tourists and almost without cars.

Rue de la Huchette is another narrow street. It is off the Boulevard Saint-Michel just before it reaches the river. Elliot Paul, an American newspaperman born in Malden, Massachusetts, lived here on and off for eighteen years, in the twenties and thirties. He wrote one of the classic books about Paris, confining it mostly to this one road, some 280m, or 300yd long. He wrote with tenderness and affection about the people who lived here, the shopkeepers, hotel-keepers, priests, wives, workers, businessmen, and called his book simply *A Narrow Street*.

The Rue de la Huchette is much more touristy these days, with aromatic smells from *suvlaki*, marinated lamb on skewers, being grilled on the pavement outside the Greek and North African restaurants that have chosen to open here. But some things are unaltered. You can still look into the dark doorway of No 10, at the murky passage below old wooden beams, that Napoleon tramped along every day, when he stayed here on one of his first visits to Paris in 1795, unknown and hard-up. It was a cheap hotel then. Further down, the Théâtre de la Huchette is still in business as the tiniest of theatres. It has only eighty-five seats and has been producing Ionesco's one-act plays at every performance for thirty years or more. The management justify this

policy by quoting Ionesco's comment that a big success in a little theatre is worth more than a small success in a big theatre.

Up in the north of Paris, in a seedy district by the Gare du Nord, is another unique theatre, one of the most advanced centres of dramatic art in the world. It is an old local music-hall, built in 1876 and called the *Bouffes du Nord*. Yvette Guilbert, the famous star of the 'café-concerts' in Paris at the turn of the nineteenth century, made her début here when she was only eighteen, but as a straight actress. It was not a success and she went on to find her real calling as a cabaret singer, wearing her long black gloves, immortalised in Toulouse-Lautrec's paintings and posters.

I made my début at the Bouffes du Nord in a play by Alexandre Dumas . . . dressed in a costume hired for three francs, with a little crown on my head that tipped sideways comically every time I moved. I will never forget that opening night, my fear of going on and my happiness once it was all over.
Yvette Guilbert, *The Song of My Life*

The appearance of the theatre has not changed all that much since Yvette Guilbert was such a flop there, but the productions are now acclaimed in London and New York, as well as all over France. You can get tickets, if you book long enough in advance, but seats are not reserved. Everyone queues outside, wet or fine, for an hour or more in order to get in and squeeze into a place on one of the tightly packed hard benches. This is not a plushy comfortable theatre, nor is there a bar, yet every production is sold out. The beauty and brilliance of the staging and the living immediacy of the performances at the Bouffes du Nord make going to ordinary commercial theatres like eating processed food.

Since 1974 the theatre has been run by the English theatre director Peter Brook, as his international centre of theatrical production. Brook is dedicated and inspired. There are no set patterns in the way he works. Every performance at his theatre is a new one, no matter how long the show has been running, as he encourages actors and actresses to be awake and conscious to the mood of the moment every time they go on stage. His most challenging production is the nine-hour cycle of *The*

Mahabharata, the great epic Sanskrit poem of Hinduism. A year after running at the Bouffes du Nord in a French translation, the huge multi-racial cast went over to New York, where it was staged in English during the latter part of 1987, well away from Broadway of course, at the grand old Majestic Theatre in Brooklyn, brought back to life and proudly restored for this event.

Trains from the Gare du Nord, next to Peter Brook's theatre, leave for the dull flatlands of the north of France and take businessmen to Lille, the commercial and industrial centre near the Belgian frontier. People leaving from the Gare de Lyon, on the other side of Paris, are more likely to be in holiday mood, going south to lie in the sun by the Mediterranean. Early in the century, at the onset of winter, the rich took *Le Train Bleu*, leaving the cold of Paris behind, to travel south overnight in a comfortable wagon-lit. The whole occasion called for a grand dinner beforehand, to help them sleep on the journey. So the Gare de Lyon was given the most fabulous station restaurant. It is still there, an unchanged anachronism, looking like a film set for the ball scene in *My Fair Lady*.

The biggest chandeliers most of us have ever seen, more lavish even than the ones in the Opéra, light up gilded columns and snow-white tablecloths. The buttoned leather armchairs could have come straight from an Establishment club in St James's in London, except that these are in much better condition. The walls and ceiling are covered with scenes of debonair people travelling south to the Côte d'Azur, men with straw hats, women with long romantic dresses, the *Train Bleu* itself, with its twenty-six coaches and puffing steam-engine.

The restaurant was named *Le Train Bleu*, after the famous train, when it was opened in 1901 by the President of France himself, Émile Loubet. This was the Belle Époque in France, the Edwardian period in Britain, the last generation for which life was carefree and relaxed, if you had enough money, before the thunderclouds of World War I darkened the scene. In 1972, seventy years after it was first opened, the Train Bleu restaurant at the Gare de Lyon was officially declared a national monument, which in the last decades of the twentieth century, puts it firmly in its place.

Thirty years ago the Marais was the most secret part of Paris, a dirty dark labyrinth of narrow streets, a mysterious city within

a city, like the souks of Marrakesh. No tourists came here. It was easy to get lost, seemingly dangerous and infested, living up to its name, which means a marsh or a bog. Not nowadays a precisely defined area, the Marais takes in the 3rd and 4th *arrondissements*, forming a triangle roughly bounded by the Hôtel de Ville to the south, the Place de la République to the north and the Place de la Bastille to the south-east.

From the fifteenth to the end of the seventeenth century, the centre of this district became more and more the fashionable place to live. Rich nobles had their mansions built here, with courtyards and formal gardens, designed by the best architects. These are the great *hôtels*, a word sometimes confusing to foreign visitors, as long before it was used to describe a place that lets rooms to travellers, *hôtel* meant a fine spacious townhouse.

Fashionable districts change from time to time in most cities. In the eighteenth century in Paris, the rich moved further west and the Marais went into a decline. The great houses fell into disrepair. In the second half of the nineteenth century, Haussmann who was busy replanning the rest of the city hardly bothered with the Marais and it was left as a dilapidated quarter for tradesmen and small factories, with some of the jewels of Parisian architecture used as warehouses.

In 1959 de Gaulle appointed the writer André Malraux as Minister of Culture. A few years later when the Marais was threatened with major post-war redevelopment, Malraux was determined to save its beautiful buildings by turning it into a conservation area. Paris woke up to the character and charm of this old district in the heart of the city. Prices went up. Splendid *hôtels* were restored and converted into expensive apartments. The beautiful Place des Vosges became one of the most sought after places to live in. But the historical labyrinth is still there and fascinating to walk through. For in any of these narrow streets, visitors can discover for themselves some of the secrets of Paris.

More than a hundred of the gracious *hôtels* of the Marais have survived, some built in the seventeenth century by the greatest architects of France. A few can be visited as they have been acquired as museums. Ten years were devoted to turning the Hôtel Salé in the Rue de Thorigny into the Picasso Museum,

described elsewhere in this book, and it was time well spent.

Picasso deservedly draws the crowds, so hardly anyone thinks of visiting the beautiful but much smaller house only a couple of minutes' walk away. This was built in 1685 and has a special quality, since it was designed by Libéral Bruant, the architect of Les Invalides, for his own personal use. A modest house by the standards of the Marais, there is an exquisite simplicity about it, a great architect building for himself. The house stands on a corner at 1 Rue de la Perle and is unexpectedly used now as a museum of locks, so it is open to the public. In passing, the locks are worth looking at too. They were made by master craftsmen dedicated to combining beauty with function. Here are locks going back to the fifteenth century, the lock specially designed for one of Marie-Antoinette's apartments and the symbolic gold key to the City of Paris.

Anywhere in the Marais you can look into intimate secluded courtyards, overhung with trees and ivy, offering a momentary glimpse into other people's lives. The second courtyard to the right within the Hôtel de Rohan at 87 Rue Vieille-du-Temple contains an astounding piece of sculpture from the early eighteenth century. Over the gateway leading to the stables, Robert Le Lorrain has given stone incredible life in a bas-relief of the four Horses of Apollo being watered by servants. Even in Paris, where there is so much, this is one of the finest things to see, yet few people ever come here.

Parisians can be intensely French (and they often are) but Paris itself is cosmopolitan, with something to offer people from almost anywhere, if they know where to look for it. Homesick New Yorkers can even find a scaled-down Statue of Liberty below the Pont Mirabeau, a couple of kilometres, less than a mile-and-half downstream from the Eiffel Tower. It was donated in 1885 by US exiles living in Paris, a piquant reversal of generosity, since the Statue of Liberty in New York Harbour was paid for by the French. They will find dry martinis 'just like home' in the Rue Daunou, near the Opéra, at Harry's Bar, with a deadpan welcome from Andy MacElhone, son of the original Harry, the archetypal New York barman.

For Londoners there is a mock-up of a Victorian pub, the Sir Winston Churchill, at 5 Rue de Presbourg, near the Étoile. Glass doors are dutifully etched *Saloon Bar* and *Private Bar*,

A secret courtyard in the Marais

even if they do both lead to the same bar. The effect is not altogether convincing, perhaps because they serve afternoon tea on the terrace outside.

Italians can sniff at salamis and mozzarellas hanging up in the *Village Italien* in the Boulevard du Temple, near the Place de la République. Japanese can try out the imitation of a 'teahouse of the August moon' in the Pagode, the exotic cinema in the 7th *arrondissement*. Dutch visitors can get a hint of Amsterdam from the tree-lined banks and hump-backed bridges along the Saint-Martin Canal, where it runs north from the Square Frédéric-Lemaître. Marxists can commune with the familiar profile of Lenin, carved on a plaque outside the apartment block at No 4 Rue Marie-Rose, where he lived from 1909–12, and even visit the Lenin Museum in his old apartment, if they are on good terms with the Soviet Embassy. And there is an unusually elegant *synagogue* at 10 Rue Pavée in the Marais, designed by Hector Guimard, no less, who designed the original art nouveau Métro entrances.

I hope this last chapter of *Paris: The Essential City* will lead you to places you might not have found for yourself and which you may come to treasure for some intimate, intriguing and magical moments you have spent in Paris, a city that offers more diverse pleasures than most other places in the world.

There is never any ending to Paris and the memory of each person who has lived in it differs from that of any other. We always returned to it no matter who we were or how it was changed or with what difficulties, or ease, it could be reached. Paris was always worth it and you received return for whatever you brought to it. But this is how Paris was in the early days when we were very poor and very happy.

Ernest Hemingway, *A Moveable Feast*

INDEX

Note: Restaurants are grouped together under *Restaurants*, cafés under *Cafés*. Streets are listed under *Rue*, squares under *Place*. **Bold** numbers show main references to a subject and also pages on which photographs appear. *Italic* numbers are for quotations. The orientation map is on pages 12-13.

Debussy, Claude, 81, 88
'Déjeuner sur l'herbe', 36, 50
Delacroix, Eugène, 30, 129, 154, 156, 179, 184
  Museum, 142, 179
Delaunay, Robert, 161, 176
Delius, 79
'Demoiselles d'Avignon, Les', 45, 48, 49
Descartes, René, 169
Desmoulins, Camille, 125
Diaghilev, Serge, 10, 86
Dickens, Charles, *61*, 66, 69, *105*, *123*
Diderot, Denis, *125*
Dior, Christian, 109, 113
Duchamp, Marcel, 29
Dufy, Raoul, 20, 161, 176
Duncan, Isadora, 50
Dupré, Marcel, 88, 89
Duras, Marguerite, 169

École des Beaux-Arts, see Beaux-Arts
École Militaire, 144
Edward VII, 160
Église de Dôme, 169, 170
Eiffel, Gustave, 159, 160
Eiffel Tower, 37, 66, 144, 148, 157, **159-161**, 175, 176
Eisenstein, 47
Eliot, T. S., 70
Epstein, Jacob, 130
Ernst, Max, 40
Escoffier, Auguste, 101, 106
Étoile, 135, 145, 170-1

Falla, Manuel de, 47, 86
Fauré, Gabriel, 79, 89
fauvism, 20
Fête de la Musique, **87,** 92
Fête Nationale, see *quatorze juillet*
Fitzgerald, Scott, 11, 47, **71-2,** 73, 140

Flaubert, Gustave, 65, 66, 105, 120
Folies, Bergère, 115
France, Anatole, 156
Franck, César, 88
Françoise I, 27, 28
Franco-Prussian War, 172
Franklin, Benjamin, 10, 136
French Revolution, 20, 125, 137, 164, 166
Freud, Sigmund, 10

Gabriel, Ange-Jacques, 136
Gaillard, Agathe, photographic gallery, 52
Gandhi, Mahatma, 164
Garbo, Greta, 140
Gare de l'Arsenal, 147
Gare de Lyon, 186
Gare Montparnasse, 172
Gare du Nord, 185, 186
Gare d'Orsay, 32, **54-5**
Garnier, Charles, 85
Gaulle, General de, 144, 170, 187
Gault and Millau, 106, *140*
Genitron, The, 41
Gershwin, George, 79-80
Giacometti, Alberto, 116
Gibbon, Edward, *151*
Gillespie, Dizzy, 92
Giverny, 36, 177, 178
Gluck, Christoph, 83
Goldwyn, Sam, 140
Goncourt, Journal des, 66
Gounod, Charles, 121
'Grand Hotels', 16
Gris, Juan, 43, 70
Guerlain perfumery, 108
'Guernica', 48
Guilbert, Yvette, 43, *185*
Guimard, Hector, 22, 36, 43, 190

Halles, Les, 102
Hardouin-Mansart, Jules, 139,